Bay *and* Her Boys

Bay *and* Her Boys

Unexpected Lessons I Learned as a (Single) Mom

BAY BUCHANAN

Da Capo

LIFE
LONG

A Member of the Perseus Books Group

Editorial production by *Marra*thon Production services. www.marrathon.net

Design by Jane Raese
Set in 12-point Bulmer

Library of Congress Cataloging-in-Publication Data is available for this book.

ISBN 978-0-7382-1513-6
ISBN 978-0-7382-1576-1 (e-Book)

First Da Capo Press edition 2012

Many of the designations used by manufacturers and sellers to distinguish their products are claimed as trademarks. Where those designations appear in this book and Da Capo Press was aware of a trademark claim, the designations have been printed in initial capital letters.

Da Capo Press books are available at special discounts for bulk purchases in the U.S. by corporations, institutions, and other organizations. For more information, please contact the Special Markets Department at the Perseus Books Group, 2300 Chestnut Street, Suite 200, Philadelphia, PA, 19103, or call (800) 810-4145, ext. 5000, or e-mail special.markets@perseusbooks.com.

10 9 8 7 6 5 4 3 2 1

TO WALT,

a single dad who has always been there for his children
and is now always there for me

Contents

Introduction

Shortly after I became a single mom I began to take note of a continual stream of bad information coming my way. New studies were constantly being released on the impact that fatherless homes had on children—and I'd watch fellow conservatives take to the talk shows, armed with the latest statistics, to make their case. *The evidence is overwhelming,* they would argue, *a dad in the home is critical to the healthy development of his children.* The picture they painted was frightening. I'd start to worry all over again that I couldn't give my kids a childhood as good as my own.

Meanwhile, I'd watch feminists comment that the rising number of female-headed homes was, on one hand, good news. *Proof,* they maintained, *that you don't need a man to have a family.* But when asked to address the awful financial and emotional consequences this new living arrangement had on kids, they spoke about victimhood and the need for government to step in to help these women and children.

Neither side offered any message of hope or encouragement that I could succeed in spite of the difficulties I was facing.

The facts were irrefutable—I knew that. They were supported by decades of research: kids raised by single parents don't fare nearly as well as those raised in traditional two-parent families. They are far more likely to abuse drugs, do poorly in school, and serve time in jail;*

Maggie Gallagher, "Why Marriage Matters: The Case for Normal Marriage," Testimony Before the U.S. Senate Subcommittee on the Constitution, Civil Rights, and they are more likely to be chronically ill, suffer from depression, and be sexually promiscuous. And they're more likely to become single parents themselves.

My own childhood had taught me the vital role that fathers play in their kids' lives. But that was no longer an option for my family— my husband had left and that path was closed to us. What was I supposed to do? Give up? Where was the advice, the guidance, the assurance that, if I did my part, my kids could make it, that they could beat the odds?

My divorce devastated me, but my kids were counting on me. I was their mom—I couldn't let them down. Billy, Tommy, and Stuart were my boys, and it was my job to see that they thrived. So I buried my fears deep inside and did the only thing I could: I made a rock-solid commitment to my three sons to put them first in my life and to always be there for them. I would give them a great childhood, a close family, and a bright future. That was my job. So that's what I'd do.

Along the way I learned it can be done. We single moms can compensate for the lack of a dad in our homes. We can handle the amazing challenge of being a parent alone. We can give our kids a healthy, happy childhood and the tools they need to thrive throughout their lives.

Property Rights Hearing: "What Is Needed to Defend the Bipartisan Defense of Marriage Act of 1996?," September 4, 2003, http://www.marriagedebate.com/pdf/SenateSept42003.pdf.

*"Adoption Fact Sheet," ItsAboutLove.org, https://itsaboutlove.org/ial/ct/eng/site/adopting-families/adoption-basics/adoption-fact-sheet/; "We now have an enormous amount of research on divorce and children, all pointing to the same stubborn truth: Kids suffer when moms and dads split up." Amy Desai, "How Could Divorce Affect My Kids?," Focus on the Family, http://www.focusonthefamily.com/marriage/divorce_and_infidelity/should_i_get_a_divorce/how_could_divorce_affect_my_kids.aspx; Erica Williams, "Children in Single Parent Homes and Emotional Problems," The Hilltop, February 6, 2003, http://www.thehilltoponline.com/2.4839/children-in-single-parent-homes-and-emotional-problems-1.472758.

But I didn't hear this message when I was raising my kids—and I worry that millions of single moms across America today aren't hearing it either. We can talk about the importance of marriage and fathers all we want—and I'd agree with every word—but we can't forget about the eighteen million kids whose fathers no longer live in their homes. Today single mothers are raising nearly one-fourth of our nation's children. These moms need to know that they can do it, that their kids can make it. They need the hope and courage that comes from knowing that it can be done—that they too can give their kids the kind of foundation in life that comes from being raised inside a strong, caring family.

It is a rough going, I know only too well, but as generations of women have proven, we have an infinite reservoir of strength within us. We just need to tap into it. Single moms are some of the toughest, most resourceful, no-nonsense people I know. Those who aren't need to get there.

What's more, the public dialogue needs to change. It's time for a heavy dose of honesty about the responsibility of motherhood, greater appreciation for the strength of women, and some solid guidance on how to be a successful single mom.

This book is the first step by this conservative to be there for these women—to stand with them, inspire them, and arm them with tools that will help them give their children the opportunity to be the men and women they were meant to be.

My Rules for Successful Parenting

Some argue that women shouldn't settle for being "just" a wife or a mom. We need to pursue our own interests, do something significant in our own right, be defined by our own accomplishments. Those people are flat-out wrong. They lack an understanding of the great wonders of being a mom and the immeasurable rewards of being a good one. There is no greater accomplishment. It takes an unshakable commitment to your kids and a willingness to sacrifice everything for them, but these are our kids we're talking about—and there is nothing more important.

I've had any number of professional titles in my life—and even more jobs—but the best of them and the one I am most proud to be called is the mother of my three boys. Were my kids perfect? Far from it. Did I make mistakes? I sure did (and you'll read about them). But we were a family, just the four of us. Together we faced whatever life sent our way, and my boys grew up to be fine young men. It was a great life, and I tell you all about it in this book. And I pull no punches. I just tell it like it was. *Bay and Her Boys* is my story—the good, the bad, and the ugly.

I wrote this book to give an honest but entirely hopeful message to single moms. But the message works for all parents. *We* are responsible for our children. It's our job to see that our kids make it. It is tough and, at times, brutally difficult, but we can do it, and we can do it well. We can succeed, and for the sake of our kids, we must. Our kids deserve a fighting chance, and only we can give it to them. What's more, the ride can be so much fun that you'd never want to miss it.

Bay and Her Boys offers a guide on how to survive the hard days, how to do it alone, and how to keep the kids in line. I tell you what worked for me, what I learned along the way, and how I kept on going. I talk about the challenges and the sacrifices, the joys and the laughs. And I lay out my eight rules for single parenting—one for every chapter.

But as I wrote this book I often thought of single dads struggling just as I had—and of married women who in many respects live my life because their husbands are away so much. And as I put words to my rules I realized that they are the basic principles of good parenting—whether you're doing it alone or not. So although I tell my story from the perspective of a single mom, the lessons within are for anyone who is a parent—or ever wants to be.

Each child is different, as is every parent, so it is up to you to determine the best way to apply these rules to your family. The key is simply to commit yourself to them—then make them work for your kids. No matter what your situation is as a parent, this book will show you how to take charge of your life, create a close family bond, and provide the warm, supportive home your kids need—all the while making the best job you'll ever have a little easier.

Bay *and* Her Boys

My Boys

I've scattered dozens of stories about my three throughout this book. In the hope of helping you distinguish one son from another, here is a short description of each of them.

Billy, My Oldest

Back in January of 1983, when Billy was born, I was Treasurer of the United States. National radio took note. All day long they announced, "Today, the U.S. Treasurer has issued a new *bill!*" and went on to report the birth of my son. I loved it but nowhere near as much as I loved having this child come into my life. I had worried I'd never have the chance to be a mom, and here I was. It was glorious.

Billy laughed and smiled through infancy, was inquisitive and talkative as a toddler, and always loved to learn. As soon as he left the crib we would lie in his bed at night and read books. When I was too exhausted to keep going, he read them to me. He had the books memorized.

He was the perfect child right up until the day he turned thirteen. It was then, I'm certain, that the teen fairy visited him at night to instruct him on the rules of being a teenager. He took to the lesson well, and the next six years were packed with attitude. But Billy excelled as both a student and an athlete, even as he turned arguing with his mother into an art form.

Billy was remarkably self-motivated, an incredibly hard worker, and a fantastic role model for his brothers. He inspired them to live better, aim higher, and never give up. He was a gift to this single mom.

Today Billy is finishing his third year at Stanford Law School and is married to Morgan. They have two beautiful children.

Tommy, My Middle Child

Tommy was born when Billy was just short of two years old. He was a fiercely independent, highly spirited child who was a born leader and a natural athlete. He loved friends and adventure, and he was never far from either.

At amusement parks Tommy would go in search of the most terrifying roller coasters and most frightening water slides and begin there. On a dude ranch vacation, where we'd go horseback riding twice a day, Tommy would always get in the "experienced riders" line. Even though he had spent little time on the back of a horse, he wasn't going to pass up the challenge and had absolute confidence he could do it. It took him a couple tries to pass the pretest, but then he was galloping through the woods with the best of them. This middle son pushed his older brother into a far more daring life than Billy would have ever chosen for himself. Never willing to turn down a dare from the younger sibling, Billy could always be found in line right behind Tommy.

As a teenager Tommy was an easygoing fella who believed his role in life was to test the rules and push the envelope. For years he gave me a run for my money, but he did it with a smile. In spite of my worries I always knew Tommy loved and respected me—he never let me think otherwise.

Today Tommy is a research analyst for a highly respected investment firm in Milwaukee, Wisconsin. He is married to Kira, and they have one wonderful little boy and, at the time of this writing, are expecting another.

Stuart, My Babe

I was three months pregnant with Stuart when his dad left our home. When he was born, Billy was not yet five years old, Tommy was three, and I was in the midst of some of the toughest days of my life. He was a shy, quiet, easy child who attached himself to me from the get-go—as well he should. He was my Babe.

Early in life Stuart became a close ally of his brother Tommy. My second son always needed to be the boss, and because that didn't work with Billy, he turned to his younger sibling, who adored Tommy and loved being part of his world.

As he grew older Stuart became his own person. Persuasion and coercion had little to no influence over the kid, and threats were no more effective. He just did his own thing. But he had fantastic friends, interesting hobbies, and an amazing sense of humor, which he used to entertain friends and teachers alike. Although he was remarkably smart, Stuart found school boring, and he didn't do boring. He did, however, become a fine writer, as you will see for yourself. Today Stuart lives in Provo, Utah, where he's working his way through college at his own pace, much to the chagrin of his mother.

Chapter One

A Mama Bear Is Born

I was born a Buchanan. This luck of the draw contributed enormously to who I am. I loved being part of my large rowdy family and thrived in the traditional Irish upbringing that went along with it. When I married, I took my husband Bill's last name, but professionally I remained Bay Buchanan. Once I became a mom, though, I wanted my kids to have a significant attachment to my roots as well as their dad's; I wanted them to feel "part Buchanan." So I put it right in their names. I made my maiden name the boys' middle name—for all three of them. Their last name was Jackson.

After my husband and I divorced, I fully returned to Buchanan, but my young kids were, of course, still Jacksons. I didn't like where this was headed. I wasn't about to spend the next twenty years going to the boys' parent-teacher meetings explaining that I was Ms. Buchanan and that the Jackson kid belonged to me. Forget that nonsense, I told myself. If I was going to be the one raising these kids, it was only right that people knew they were mine—right up front.

I told my attorney I wanted to hyphenate the boys' last name—change it to "Buchanan-Jackson." The two names were already there, I told him; all I wanted to do was add a little hyphen. What's the big deal? He advised against a legal battle, knowing their dad would fight me and probably win—not to mention the cost. "Don't try to change it legally, just do it," he told me. "When you enroll them in school or sports programs, just put their name down as "Buchanan-Jackson." No one will ever question you—you're their mom." It was brilliant.

Over the years school administrators would call to explain that their computers didn't provide enough spaces in the "last name" category to accommodate the boys' name. Then they would ask which half I wanted them to use. To assure they didn't push the issue I would respond indignantly, "But that's their name—you can't just drop half of it." I threw the responsibility back on them, knowing full well that they would keypunch as much as they could and then stop—maybe losing the last few letters of the Jackson part. The result was that the boys' last name effectively became Buchanan-Jackson, or Buchanan, for short. My plan worked perfectly—I never had to explain to anyone which kid was mine.

(It wasn't long before my ex found out, and he wasn't too pleased. He had his attorney send me a few letters in an effort to get me to use the boys' legal name, but I ignored them. I had a winning game and wasn't going to be distracted.)

But none of this solved the problem of the Christmas cards. How would I sign them? I'd been sending them every year since my first son was born, and I would always include a picture of the boys. When I was married, it was easy—I signed them "The Jacksons" and then listed our names. But I wasn't a Jackson anymore and the kids weren't Buchanans. This presented a dilemma. I couldn't use last names, and using only first names—Bay, Billy, Tommy, and Stuart—didn't do it for me. Somehow it didn't say "we're family"—it didn't attach them to me.

I was talking to a friend about my predicament when she said, "Just put 'Bay and her boys' on the cards. It says it all." That it did—it said it all and it said it well. I was a single mom now—and I was a proud one.

And that is where my story begins.

———

Twenty-four years ago I was thrown (*dumped* might be a more appropriate word) into the world of single parenting. I had a four-year-old, a two-year-old, and was three months pregnant with the third—all boys. I arrived in this place with no experience, no knowledge, and no idea how to succeed. I didn't even know how I was going to pay the bills. But one thing I did know—I would do right by my boys. I would figure it out, and I would succeed. They deserved that, and I had a responsibility to deliver.

Having failed to provide my kids with a father in their home, I was more determined than ever to give them a childhood as good as mine. I had loved growing up in my big, traditional Catholic clan, and I went off to college believing I had the greatest family on earth. I wanted the same kind of wonderful memories for my boys. But my dad had been a central figure in our family's dynamics. I didn't know if I could create the same magic without a father at the helm, but I was sure as heck going to try.

In my mind I was the least likely person to end up as a single mother. I believed that being divorced meant you had failed at the most important job you'd ever have. And to raise kids alone was not just unfortunate; it was tragic. In those days it was generally accepted that single moms were a sad lot, that their lives had fallen apart, and that their kids would suffer as a result. How could any of this happen to me? Nothing in my family life gave me any reason to even consider this possibility. And I had never failed at anything significant in my life. Why would I start now?

I was raised the seventh child in a family of nine, with a fully engaged dad and a stay-at-home mom. What's more, I was a church-going, traditional, conservative woman who firmly believed in the importance of the two-parent family, had always wanted a house full of kids, and fell in love with a man who shared my goals. It was so perfect. How could this go wrong? I was completely committed to my family and willing to sacrifice to make the marriage work. But there I was, after only a half-dozen years of marriage, with two (and a half) kids in tow, headed out the door of my California home to an appointment with a divorce attorney. Shame and anger consumed me as I handed him the divorce papers I'd been served, and the tears fell.

It was a sad, ignominious end to my dreams.

Before I got married, I had a dream career as Treasurer of the United States, was doing well financially, and was living in my hometown of Washington, DC. Life was good for this single gal when, out of nowhere, my old flame called "just to say hi." Bill and I had met on a California tennis court a few years earlier when I was working for Ronald Reagan's Santa Monica–based political action committee. We had an on-again-off-again relationship, which was totally off when I returned to DC with Reagan's 1980 presidential campaign. A year later, while sitting in my huge office at the Department of the Treasury, I picked up the phone, and Bill's call was put through to me. Soon after that, it was back on. We were married the following year. Six years later, he was gone.

My world had come apart. I was no more financially prepared for this development than I was emotionally. I had no job, had held no permanent position since my days at Treasury, had no savings, co-owned a heavily mortgaged home, and was deep into credit card debt. It was a precipitous fall, but I had picked up a few assets along the way and I wasn't about to lose them. "Get me the kids," I told my lawyer. "I don't care about anything else. Just get me the kids."

My dad had not approved of my marriage, so his words kept coming to mind: "If he'll leave his kids once, he'll do it again." My husband had been married before, and when he first divorced, he left behind three young boys. I never even considered history repeating itself—right down to the three boys. Chalk it up to love. But Dad saw it as likely, and he worried for his grandchildren. He knew all too well the depth of the scars that divorce can leave on kids.

When I was a teenager, late one evening I found Dad sitting alone in the dining room. He couldn't sleep and had come downstairs for a nightcap. He began to talk to me about the last time he, as a child, saw his own father. He was eleven and in fifth grade. He was living away from his Georgetown home at the time—at Mount Washington Boarding School in Baltimore. One afternoon an elderly nun found him in the cafeteria and told him his dad, "a handsome man," had come to see him. His father took him outside and told him he was leaving—leaving his wife and two sons and moving to Milwaukee.

Dad idolized his father. He said that for years after that terrible day he would search for tall, red-headed men in the hallways of his school and on the sidewalks of the city. When he spotted one, he'd race ahead to see if it might be his dad. You never forget something like that, he told me. And it appeared you never get over the pain either—you just learn to live with it.

The story broke my heart. Dad was a tough, hard-working, proud Irishman (some Scottish in there, but you didn't dare go there with him). He was a successful businessman, well respected in the community and in his church, and a coach of too many kids' basketball and football teams for me to count. Yet here he was, fifty-some years later, talking to his seventh child about the awful day his father left him. Some things just never go away.

Dad's experience haunted me in the early days of my divorce. Although my ex-husband was not disappearing altogether—he would have limited custody—my youngest would never know what it was like to have his dad living in his home, and the other two would have little to no memory of it. I knew what it was like to have two good parents in the home—knew the sense of order and security it provided. My kids would never experience this, and I feared they would feel the loss for the rest of their lives.

But Dad had turned his tragedy into a powerful commitment to never let it happen to his own kids. He vowed he would always be there for his family—and he always was. When my brother Pat wrote my father's eulogy, he titled it "The Best Man I Ever Knew." Dad was bigger than life in the eyes of his children.

As I was facing single parenting I knew I needed to make a pact like Dad's—a rock-solid commitment to be there for my kids. Every child deserves to be first in someone's life. Because I brought these little guys into this world, they would be first in my life. I would do everything in my power to give them a childhood as good as the one I had. I would give them a secure place to call home, a family life filled with love and laughter, and the absolute knowledge that there was someone who would always believe in them, and would always fight for them as they grew to be the young men they were meant to be. This I could do—and this I would do.

I would make my life their life. That is how it would be and how it should be.

The First Steps

Leaving the Past Behind

Soon after becoming a single parent I ran into an old friend whom I hadn't seen in years. She was married with kids the last time we met. "How are you?" I asked.

"Oh," she sighed, and then hesitantly added, "I'm so embarrassed to tell you, Bay. I'm divorced."

It was so hard for her to talk about it. A product of a strong Catholic family, she whispered to me that she "felt like such a failure."

I knew how she felt. But I also knew she had to get past it—and she had to do it quickly. There was too much at stake. "You're not a failure," I told her. "You can't afford to be. You're a mom!"

I was astonished at how adamant I was—almost offended that she would speak of herself as a failure. *She needs to get past the muck of the divorce,* I thought, *and start dealing with the reality of being a single parent.* Of course, it hadn't been that long since I was there—exactly where she was. And some nights I was still in that awful place. I would put the boys to sleep, do the dishes, throw a load of laundry in, then go to bed and cry. I would brave the storm all day, staying focused on the routine of a working single mom, but when the house was quiet and the lights were out, I lost the battle and the tears of divorce took over.

Even when a marriage isn't perfect—and few are—we still hold onto that which is good about it. You identify as a couple, do things as a pair, talk about your day with each other, and share stories about your children. Being part of a two-parent family lends a sense of comfort to you as well as the kids; it blankets all its members with a sense of security.

Being married is a commitment to another person, and your life is intricately tied to theirs. It becomes who you are and who you see yourself being long into the future. Even an imperfect union accomplishes this at some level.

When divorce hit, I felt as if I'd lost my identity. My dreams were shattered, my self-confidence flattened, and my plans for the future spread all over the editing room floor. I was as uncertain and confused as I had ever been. And to make matters worse, divorce had robbed me of precious memories. This painful realization hit me hard when, in the midst of the upheaval, my dad died.

His death came just three weeks after my third baby, Stuart, was born. Fortunately I was able to fly to Washington and be at his bedside for the final few days of his life. At Dad's wake—a good, old-fashioned Irish one—family and friends gathered, and the talk was all about him. The stories seemed to go on forever, including some I had never heard before. I was filled with such warm feelings as I learned how my father had touched so many lives. We laughed and cried together in celebration of the life of a man we all loved. The loss I felt was enormous, but remembering him was a great comfort and continues to be today.

That night I realized that Dad's death wasn't nearly as cruel as my divorce. Recalling the good times—the courtship, the marriage, the happier days—had become too painful for me. I wondered if it had all been an act—one long, fraudulent relationship. Maybe not, I'd switch gears and consider—maybe some of it was real. But if that were the case, when did the lies begin? When did he stop loving me? Or did he ever love me? Thinking about the good times with my ex was emotionally devastating. I couldn't keep doing this to myself. I couldn't keep thinking about my past with him, I had to forget—or at least suppress—the memories I had of the man I married. And so I did.

Moving Forward as a Proud Single Mom

When I ran into my friend on the street, I understood exactly how she felt. But deep inside I knew there was life after divorce—a good life. I had survived the shock and the hurt, and I was determined not to let the bitterness and loneliness consume me. Whenever I thought I was losing the battle, I would peek in the kids' bedroom and look at those sweet sleeping faces. These little guys were counting on me, and I wasn't going to let them down. There was too much at stake for me to fail, so I started to think of a different future, one that was good and bright and full of fun. And I embraced it. It was all about kids, and although it was full of uncertainty, it would be a great adventure for all four of us—I'd make certain of it.

As the months passed I began to see great benefits to my new approach to life. Good things were happening to me and my family. Seeing my friend, in all her grief and shame, made me reflect on these changes. I thought about how I had moved away from the misery of divorce, which unfortunately still consumed her, to where I was now: a fighting, surviving single mom. My thoughts were no longer about me and my lost dreams; they were about the three little guys under the age of five who were completely dependent on me. I had learned that the anger and self-pity weren't helping any of us, so I had swallowed my pride and reined in my emotions.

My boys' childhood—the one I promised would be as good as my own—was in my hands. They were relying on me for a good life, one that would give them a chance at being exactly who they were meant to be. I planned to succeed. The past no longer had a hold on me—the future was too important.

Yes, I had lost my old identity. But I was acquiring a new one, and it fit well. It didn't matter what others thought anymore. I was a mom—with all the responsibility that comes with that great title. So what if friends felt awkward, acquaintances avoided me in the grocery store, or teachers whispered behind my back? What did I care that those so-called smart people on television were calling single mothers some kind of needy victims, giving our kids little chance to succeed? They didn't know me or my kids. I wasn't going to let anyone make me feel ashamed nor would I accept their pity. To succeed at this job—to do it well—I had to feel good about what I was doing. With the stakes as high as they were, I couldn't afford to let others bring me down. So I went on the offense. I stopped talking about the divorce, and when asked, I gave no details. And when I ran into old friends, I'd tell them: "I'm a single mom now!" as if I had won the lottery—and some days I thought I had.

Sure, I was on my own now. But I had always been independent— and the good news was that, unlike marriage, it didn't take two to make this new life of mine work. It only took me. There were advantages, I thought, to being a single mom, and I was going to enjoy every one of them.

Crisis happens to all of us. And you need to grieve—but you have to shove the pain deep inside of you until after hours. In the midst of so much chaos in their lives, kids desperately need an in-charge, upbeat, all-is-well kind of parent. As the days pass and you manage to get into a routine that works for you and the kids, the evenings will take care of themselves. More and more frequently you'll go to bed so exhausted that the sleep will come before the sadness can hit.

To be a good mom you need to drop the things of the past; forget all the "what ifs," the "what weres," and the "what might have beens"; and turn your attention to being the person you are now: a single mom. Don't let the bad that happened consume you. Don't spend a lot of time in yesterday. And it doesn't matter how you ended up as a single parent—divorce, out-of-wedlock birth, single adoption, or widowed. You're in a new world now, and if you're going to carry the baggage of the past into it, you can't live it well.

Your kids need you to be a responsible adult, a take-charge person. On this point you are totally accountable. Their lives depend on you getting it together and assuring them, in both word and deed, that everything is under control.

Although the days ahead will be challenging and at times overwhelming, they will also be full of fun and forever rewarding if you do it right. It's time to move forward and throw yourself into life as a single mom—it'll make you a stronger, better person, so what are you waiting for?

Don't Sweat the Small Stuff

For six months or so after the divorce I found that it was often the simplest things that set me back. Taking out the trash, for instance, bothered me for months—it was a constant little reminder, like a sharp jab to my side, that this had been *his* job, and now it was *mine*. Then I'd recall that all his chores were now mine, and my mood would darken.

I found this to be especially true when it came to the car. I can't explain why, but it took me years to get over the fact that I was now responsible for getting the car inspected and the oil changed. My ex had taken pride in keeping the cars serviced, but that too was now up to me. I hated doing it, and it took way too long before I accomplished these simple tasks without my blood pressure ticking up a notch or two.

Then there were our friends. The ones we had in common—the couples we would occasionally join for some Mexican food and a movie. Or maybe we'd get the families together for hamburgers and hot dogs. Once I was divorced, they never called again.

It is an amazing phenomenon, actually. I've spoken to dozens of single parents, and they all say the same thing: when they became single, their social life went the way of their marriage—it vanished. I had a hard time with this at first. I wasn't a high-maintenance friend, but I used to think it would be fun if one of these couples would invite the kids and me over for a Sunday dinner. It never happened.

I was baffled. Initially I would think, *What is this? Do they think I'm going to make a play for their husband?* A ridiculous reaction, I admit, but none of it made any sense to me.

Looking back I am far more sympathetic to their plight, something I didn't give a moment's thought to at the time. It's not as if these friends no longer liked me—or you if you've had this same experience. They just felt awkward around us and didn't know what to say, so they avoided us. Though it was human nature, it hurt just the same. And we already had our fill of that stuff.

Also in their defense, couples usually socialize with couples—when you stop being part of one, you no longer fit the mold. It's not you— it's your marital status that puts you outside their comfort zone. So don't let it get you down. Their get-togethers are boring without you anyhow. At least's that's what I told myself.

Those early days of single parenting are full of unwelcomed demands and unpleasant situations. But as time passes, what seemed so difficult at first (like taking out the trash) becomes part of your routine. Likewise, your social circle fills up with little league parents and neighbors with kids. Just hang in there—give yourself time to adjust to this new life. It will happen.

There are, however, a few situations that you'll need to nip in the bud if your goal is to move forward.

First is the friend who feels compelled to tell you everything they know about your ex's latest activities. I had such a friend.

Six months after my ex walked into the sunset I invited this individual, his family, and others over for dinner. It was Christmas and I wanted the boys to be surrounded by the same folks with whom we'd always shared this holiday. Their dad came over for a few hours in the early morning, and close family friends filled the house most of the afternoon. As others cleaned up the kitchen or played with the boys, I found myself alone in the living room as this friend put together one of the kids' new toys. It was then that he took it upon himself to tell me that the father of my boys had found a "nice gal"—a nurse, he volunteered—who seemed really good for him. He kept talking about her, but it didn't matter. The walls around me had collapsed and I couldn't hear or talk. Stuart was thirteen days old and I was emotionally frail. I just didn't know how frail until that moment. I left my guests, went to my bedroom with my baby, and cried uncontrollably for hours. I never even said goodbye to my guests.

No harm was intended; I knew that. But I chose never to socialize with this fine couple again—it was too high risk. I learned that horrible Christmas day that divorce sometimes requires a separation of friends as well as assets. This family would go with him. I needed to move to safer ground.

Second is the close confidante who willingly listens to you talk for hours about your marriage and divorce. She may even encourage the conversation and always takes your side. Who wouldn't like this? And who doesn't need a shoulder to cry on in the early days? But you can't keep it up. You'll never get rid of the bitterness if you keep talking about it for months—or years. You have to cut these conversations short as quickly as possible. If your friend brings up the topic, tell her you don't want to go there anymore. That chapter of your life is over, so you need to close the book on it.

Like I said, sometimes when you are making real progress with the big issues, the small things make you stumble and fall. It happens to us all. Just get up, dust yourself off, and move forward. Once you are a fully engaged single mom, you will look back on these days and see how far you've come, how strong you are, and how good it feels to be the mom your kids deserve.

Facing the Tougher Adjustments

As the months passed I grew comfortable being a single mom, but there were some adjustments I was never able to make. Where other single parents seemed to take them in stride, I never did. I just had to learn to deal with them as best I could, but it didn't come easy—not ever.

Take school programs, for instance, the ones parents are expected to attend. I would get the boys ready, and with excitement in the air, we would head off to school for a fun afternoon or evening. The children involved would go to their classrooms to get ready, and I'd take a seat in the audience with the other kid or two. Then I'd see him a few rows over—my ex—sitting with another woman by his side.

In a matter of moments I'd become nauseous and was moved to the brink of tears. It was a physical reaction that I couldn't overcome—

a bit of the heartbreak that never healed. When the kids sitting with me saw him, they'd be so happy and run over to be with him. Now that that sword was dug in deep, I'd think, why not twist it a bit?

All I could do was take deep breaths, put on a fake smile, and count the minutes until I could get out of there. I would have preferred a good root canal to attending these events.

Then there was coping with a sick or hurt child—on my own. It always made me feel so inadequate, so needy, so depressed that I had to go through the tough, scary hours of worrying how serious the illness, or how bad the injury, without a partner.

At midnight on that same horrible Christmas I mentioned earlier, I was taking a long, hot recuperative shower when my three-year-old, Tommy, came into the bathroom to tell me he couldn't breathe. Middle of the night, three babies, a medical emergency—and a dad nowhere to be found. Times like this seemed to give those bad feelings buried deep within me an opportunity to just have at it. It was the harsh reality that it was just me now, and I'd get angry. But I had to resist. I would tell myself to focus on being there for the kids, to take care of them, and to more fully appreciate having them in my life—and to fight the bitterness I felt because no one was there for me.

That night I woke up a friend from church and asked if she would come over and watch two boys, including my two-week-old infant, while I took the third to the hospital.

Much to my good fortune, a few years later a lady named Pam and her family moved into the house three down from ours. We became best friends, and Pam and her husband were always there to help me when one adult was not enough, something for which I'll be forever grateful. (In hindsight I should have asked Pam to go to the kids' programs with me. I may have solved that problem as well!)

Life as a single mom is an experience that tests every part of you. Expect the unexpected, and take it as it comes. Don't let the tough stuff keep you down. Some of these adjustments may never sit well with you, but that's okay. You just need to learn to cope—preferably with a smile.

The Bottom Line

By the time he was in college, my second son, Tommy (a boy who, at the age of three, attempted a hostile takeover of the family), began to refer to me as the Mama Bear. He was right—this is exactly what I had become. It didn't happen overnight, but the seeds were planted more than twenty years earlier—not when I became a single mom but when I decided what kind of single mom I would be.

I call it Rule #1: "You're a Single Mom—Take Charge." No matter how devastating the upheaval, how deep your pain, or even how frightening the road ahead, remember that there is no one your kids need more than you. Their dad is gone, their hearts are broken, and they are scared. They can't start to heal until they know that you are okay. You have to take charge of your life—and theirs. You have to let them know that no matter what, you will figure it out, make it work, and always be there for them, and then prove that you mean it every single day.

You are the head of your family. The responsibility is enormous, as is the challenge. But you can do it—never think otherwise. Believe in yourself. Your kids need to know you are up to the job of being their mom so they can go back to being children. Be proud. Be strong. And never let anyone or anything come between you and your kids—be their Mama Bear.

Chapter Two

Let Their Dad
Be Their Dad

I was born into a full house—with five older brothers and a sister. (Two more brothers came along later.) My birth was not an easy one, and there was some concern I might not make it. It was the Christmas season, and when all turned out well, my dad, with a heart full of thanks, named me Angela Marie, "angel of Mary." But we were a nickname family, and I got mine when I came home from the hospital. Brother Jack, my Irish twin (he was less than a year older than me) couldn't say "baby." He said, "bay-bay." The big brothers picked it up and ran with it. They called me Bay and it stuck.

Thirty years later I was the treasurer of Ronald Reagan's presidential campaign, but I was still called "Bay." I had worked as an accountant for his 1976 primary challenge to President Ford and then spent the next three years as the controller of his political action committee. When he decided to make another run at the presidency, I set my sights on the campaign treasurer's job. It was a prominent position, and I was young and female, so it was a hard sell. In those days, not much different than now, big titles went to big names, and staffers did the work. That wasn't happening to me. I was relentless in my effort to land both the job and the title—and I succeeded.

A wonderful little perk came with the package. Federal law required that the name of the treasurer be included in a campaign's disclaimer. Here's how it read: "Paid for by Reagan for President; Paul Laxalt, Chairman; Bay Buchanan, Treasurer." Pretty sweet, huh? Admittedly it was only found in small print in out-of-the-way places on campaign brochures and the like, but on television and radio ads it was read out loud. I loved it. Dad, however, did not share my enthusiasm.

It was his custom to watch a few hours of television with my mom every night after dinner. During one such occasion he saw a Reagan political commercial and heard the glorious words: "Paid for by Reagan for President . . . Bay Buchanan, Treasurer." He called the next day. "You can't use your nickname!" he told me. "You have to use your Christian name on official documents and in public venues." He then went on about how beautiful a name Angela Marie was and added, with a touch of ridicule, "As for 'Bay,' people are just going to think it's a typo for 'Ray' and that you're a man." He had a point. But I held my ground.

Reagan won, and upon taking office in January of 1981, he named me Treasurer of the United States. At age thirty-two I was—and remain today—the youngest person to have ever held that office. As the nation's Treasurer my signature would appear on the front, bottom, left-hand corner of all newly printed bills. (The signature of Donald T. Regan, the president's designated Secretary, also known as the Secretary of the Treasury, would appear opposite mine on the right-hand corner.)

These were exciting days for my family, but they were not without some anxious moments. A few weeks after the announcement Dad had a late-night panic attack. "She'll put it on the dollar bill," he told Mom. "She'll put 'Bay' on the dollar bill!"

By morning he was beside himself and instructed Mom to call me. "Tell her she can't put her nickname on the dollar bill," he said. "Tell her she has to use her Christian name."

"She's been doing things her own way since she was twelve," Mom responded. "What makes you think she'll change now?"

Dad, a partner in a prominent accounting firm, left for work, but by lunch he was back home. He had come up with a fresh approach and needed Mom's help. He told her, "Call Bay and tell her that 'as a special request' her father would like her to use her Christian name on the dollar bill." He had me. I mean, how many "special requests from your father" do daughters get? It was the only one I ever received, and I wasn't going to turn him down; it meant too much to him. Dad won this round, and as a result the name "Angela M. Buchanan" can be found on all denominations of bills printed from 1981 to the middle of 1983.

When the first "Buchanan bills"—as I like to call them—were printed, the press asked why I hadn't used the name by which I have always been known. Feeling like a teenager, I told them, "My dad asked me to use my Christian name, the one he gave me." Hey, it was the least this daughter could do for her father. And I never regretted it.

Dads can have a powerful influence over their children—just by always being there for them and always loving them. The kids will do the rest—they'll find all kinds of good ways to show they love him too.

Make no mistake: dads do matter. And when divorce happens, it takes a terrible toll on the kids. They may tell you what they know you want to hear—that they're fine—but don't believe it for a moment. The very foundation of their lives has been shaken. Their family—the primary source of their security and happiness—has been yanked out from under them. For most kids this means that their father, the man they love the most, a central figure in their lives, is gone from their home. It's a devastating blow, and it doesn't matter if the children are toddlers or teens, the wounds are real and deep. Don't let anyone tell you differently.

My boys had an older dad—he was fifty-one years old when my youngest was born—but he was a good athlete who exercised weekly and was in excellent physical condition all his life. So it was all the more shocking, twelve years after he had left our home, to get the call that he'd died of a massive heart attack. He was sixty-three.

With a heavy heart I gathered the boys together in my bedroom to tell them the sad news. Tommy was the first to respond, and he did so angrily: "First, you and Dad get divorced; now my dad dies—and I'm only fourteen! This isn't how it's supposed to be!"

This young teenager immediately connected these two awful events in his life. He understood that, together, these incidents had cheated him out of a deep and strong relationship with his dad and destroyed his dreams of getting to know his father better when he was older.

We had a good life, my boys and I, and they've done well. But the scars of divorce are still with them and will be for the rest of their lives, just as they were for my dad. I was painfully reminded of this when, wanting their insights for this book, I asked each one of them to write their thoughts about being raised without a dad in their home. Without speaking to one another, each wrote about a powerful sense of loss.

Here is how my youngest son, Stuart, who is now a twenty-three-year-old college student, put it:

My father was a great man. You can ask anyone who knew him and they would tell you of his outstanding athletic ability, genuine charity toward his fellow man, and remarkable intellect. He was loved by all because he was the first to love. But, like all men, he wasn't perfect. He made mistakes. And one mistake in particular changed my life before I was even born.

You see, while my mother was pregnant with me, my dad left. And just like that, without any say of my own, possibly the most important figure in my life was gone. That is not to say that my mom isn't perfect, because she is. But no matter how loving and understanding and strong a mother may be, no one can replace a father in a boy's life. I am not talking about how a boy loves his dad. I am talking about the role that the father plays in the lives of his children.

There is no greater method of teaching than by example. And every boy deserves to learn by observing a good father. Aside from the basics, like how to throw a football, how to reduce razor burn, or how to change a flat tire, there are essentials that a boy must learn as he grows up, things that he needs to learn from his dad. Actually, let me rephrase that: things that he wants to learn from his dad. Things like how to get the girl in your chemistry class to notice you. Things like how to throw a punch hard enough to make sure those punks at school never mess with you again. And ultimately we want to know how to raise the family we will one day have.

Can you understand what it's like for an eight-year-old boy to sit in church as they announce a father-son camping trip for the next weekend? Can you imagine how a mother feels when she has to call the father of her son's friend to ask if he might take her boy along too? Or how she feels when each one of her boys eventually gets old enough to ask, "Mom, why did Dad leave?"

As I got older my innocent acceptance of not having had a father in my home evolved. I can pinpoint the moment when I stopped being a child. I was eleven, and I was sitting in a cemetery as they lowered my father's coffin into his grave. People who I had never met before, nor ever cared to, were getting up and saying a few words about how wonderful my father was, about how he had changed their lives. I sat there and wondered what I could say if I were to stand up and share something. I sat there and thought hard. And the only thing I could come up with was "He used to call and help me with my Spanish homework."

I had the privilege of knowing my father, which, I realize, is a blessing a lot of children go without, so I'm grateful for it. What little time I did spend with him is more precious to me than all the riches in the world, more precious than anything, save time spent with my mom. For all the times I have been smacked upside the head, sent to my room, or been forced to weed the garden for hours on end, I wouldn't give up one second spent with her. That my mother succeeded in keeping my brothers and me from killing each other is remarkable, but the fact that she did so alone is nothing short of a miracle. Everything good that I will ever do can be traced back to nights spent curled up by her side as a child, sharing a bowl of popcorn and watching as John Wayne saved the day yet again. Which makes me wonder what more I would have achieved in my life had my father been there on the couch with us during those influential evenings.

Stuart is so right. No one can replace a dad. The relationship between a father and son—or a father and daughter—are undeniably special. And children know it. They want their dad around to talk and joke with, to yell with delight when he comes through the door, or wrestle him to the ground after dinner. It is a unique bond that is meant to be theirs.

Kids know instinctively that their dad belongs in their life, and they desperately want him there. This desire is so powerful that many kids of divorce hold close the dream that their folks will one day soon get back together. He may be the last man you want in your life, but he is the guy they most want in theirs.

What's more, they need him there. The evidence is overwhelming and indisputable. Children who live with both parents are far more likely to thrive than those who don't. So if your kids—for whatever reason—have no dad in their home, you have to try to give them the next best thing: their dad in their lives. No matter what you think of him, one of the best things you can do for your kids, if it's possible, is to give them memories of time spent with their dad.

So if you're a mom with most of—if not all—the burden of raising the kids on your shoulders, what are you going to do? After work, while the kids' dad is off playing tennis at the club or having dinner with his latest flame, you're refereeing fights and redoing third grade. You try not to think about him—you know doing so will keep you out of heaven. Yet the kids need him—the same guy you want attacked by a Doberman on the way to his tennis match is the guy they need in their lives.

It's a serious dilemma. You don't want anything to do with the man, but your kids love him and want to be close to him. Conflicted interests, you might say. But when it comes down to you or them— guess what? You lose; they win. Sacrifice is the central theme in the lives of all good moms. Without tons of it, you won't succeed.

So after taking control of your own life and providing your kids a safe and secure home, the most important thing you can do for your kids, without question, is give them a real shot at a solid relationship with their dad. Now, he has to do the work, but there is plenty that you can do—and must do—to create an environment that will allow this bond to flourish. You may not be able to make their dad be a great dad, but you can create a world around the kids that will give him every opportunity to be one.

Giving Your Kids a Chance for a Great Relationship with Their Dad

Let's get down to specifics. Here are five action items that you must do for your kids' sake—each one tougher than the next—to encourage this all-important relationship between their dad and them. All of this assumes, of course, that contact with their dad in no way threatens your child's physical or emotional well-being. (And for single dads, this applies to you as well: give your kids a chance to have a healthy relationship with their mom by making these five steps part of your life.)

#1. Don't Ever Let Your Kids Think They Were in Any Way Responsible for the Divorce

After the divorce my feelings were raw. Just seeing the boys' dad would flood my mind with memories of betrayal and broken promises, causing my heart to nearly break all over again. As the years passed I learned just to go cold—try to feel nothing when I was around him. The divorce had cut me to the bone, but it had done the same to the kids. They loved their dad and they loved him in their home; then something terrible had happened and he was no longer there.

They would often ask me, "Why did Dad leave, Mom? Was it because of me?" They were desperately trying to make sense of this awful turn of events and were worried that maybe they were to blame—somehow, some way they caused their dad to leave. Of course, the divorce had nothing to do with them, and it would be brutally unfair to let them think it, even for a moment. I told them again and again that they had absolutely nothing to do with the divorce. It was between their dad and me—that he just stopped loving me. He always loved them and always would.

Single parents need to constantly keep in mind—and impress upon their kids—that the divorce was not about them. Make it clear and repeat it often, like a mantra. From day one never let them think they had anything to do with this terrible upheaval in their lives. Tell them that their dad loves them, that nothing will change that—just as you love them and always will. This isn't a contest about who loves them more. Don't make it one.

If your kids are like mine, they'll then ask, "If we weren't the cause, Mom, why did Dad leave?" Give them a reason—they need to have something so they don't blame themselves. Tell them he left because he stopped loving you or you left because you stopped loving him or some equally simple explanation and never change it. Year in and year out, tell them the divorce had nothing to do with them, that their dad always loved them and always will. They can't hear it enough. You need to make certain they know this to be the rock solid truth and that they believe it with all their heart.

#2. Don't Share the Divorce's Dirty Details with Your Kids

This isn't true confessions—your kids don't need to know everything their dad did or said that offended you. And it doesn't matter if it's true. You need to protect them from the ugliness. Tell them nothing that would make them think less of their dad. Otherwise you'll undermine their respect for him, and you have no right to do that. It's your baggage, not theirs. Don't dump it on them. Don't use the divorce to pit the kids against their dad. Divorce is tough enough for them—don't make it worse.

If the kids are older, there is plenty they may already know. Don't lie to them, but don't dramatize or elaborate. If possible, reduce the conversation to telling them that these issues have nothing to do with them—mistakes were made, but they were between their dad and you. Then hit the mantra: their dad loves them, always has, and always will, just as you do.

Your ex may not be so generous of spirit and may tell stories out of school. Don't respond in kind. This is really tough, but the key is to remember that your concern is the kids. If they ask about something he said, don't lie—deflect. Something like, "That's yesterday's news with a spin, is all I can say." Or if applicable, use one of my favorites: "That's not how I remember it, but you can check the court documents for yourself when you're older."

Your goal: do no harm. Don't demonize their dad. No blame, no harsh words, no tell-all tales. Divorce sent him out of your life—don't let it send him out of theirs. Whatever you think of him, he can be a good dad. Let him have that chance, because a good dad is too precious a gift to take from your kids.

My oldest son, Billy, was in his second year at Stanford Law School when his second child—and first son—was born. He named him William Richards Jackson—Will, for short. As is my custom, I spent a week helping out Will's parents soon after he arrived. One afternoon Billy, who was studying for exams, met me for lunch and a few minutes of private time. Out of nowhere Billy said to me, "Mom, thank you for never saying anything bad about Dad. I didn't want to know—not then, not now." He loved his dad and cherished the good memories he had—so much so that the first chance he had, he honored him by naming his son after him.

Billy's dad meant the world to him—he was loved by him, knew it, and loved him back. Is it asking too much of a mom to give her kids a chance at this? I don't think so.

#3: Don't Bad-Mouth the Kids' Dad

When I asked my boys to send me their thoughts on life without a dad at home, I had no idea how difficult the reading would be. I knew the kids had suffered—I was there, I saw it up close. But when I read

Billy's account of an incident that occurred so many years ago, my heart broke.

Here is what he wrote:

When I was five or six Dad took my brother Tommy and me to the flower shop to buy some roses for Mom. I was excited—maybe they would get back together! Get remarried! This was not a new idea for me. Since I began having thoughts in my head, I pictured Dad coming home and staying. We bought the flowers. Dad took us home.

Mom was waiting outside to greet us. This was new—she never did that before. Maybe she was excited? It was Valentine's Day, after all; she could have been expecting something. Not so. She had tears in her eyes. She was upset. We all got out of the car and she ran to Dad. Instead of a hug, she hit him on the chest several times and yelled at him for bringing us home late. I think we were an hour or so late. She said, "How could you do this to me? How?" She didn't care about the flowers. He apologized and left. That ended my weekend.

Granted, that was one of the worst experiences I had as part of a divorced family.

You're probably thinking the same thing I did when I read this: what in the world was I doing? I don't remember hitting their dad. It wasn't something that had ever happened before. But I can't question Billy's description—the details seem to be seared into his memory. I, however, had buried all recollection of this evening deep in a mental file called "repressed memories," where it would have remained until I met my Maker had Billy not shaken it loose first.

Let me shed some light on the two and a half hours that preceded this incident.

The boys' dad was a trial attorney, and he had learned early in his career that when you are late for a trial, two things happened. First, you lose your case. Second, you lose your client. The lesson took, and he applied it to all aspects of his life. Although he was constantly changing the day and the time he would pick up the kids, once he let me know when he was coming, he was as prompt a person as you could meet.

That day when their dad picked up the two oldest, he told me he'd have them back at six that evening. When six o'clock came and went, I wrote it off to California freeway traffic. As the clock moved toward seven I began to panic. Half past seven I called the police and asked if they were aware of any major accidents. They told me to call local hospitals. I called every one of them. A half-hour later I called them again.

By eight-fifteen I was out of my mind. I thought of asking a friend to wait with me. I didn't want to be alone with the baby if tragic news was coming my way. But I couldn't—I thought that placing this call would somehow make my worst fears come true.

I tried to figure out why I hadn't received a call. Their dad would surely instruct medical crews to call me if he could. And both boys were able to provide enough information if someone needed to find me. What terrible thing had happened, I kept asking myself, that not one of them was able to get word to me?

It was close to eight-thirty when their dad pulled up. By now I was as close to hysterical as I would ever know. The kids came popping out of the car all excited and ran smack into a crazy lady. They had never seen me like this and never should have. I raced to hug my boys for dear life when I saw their dad and let him have it for putting me through this living nightmare. But the kids had no idea what I'd gone through; they only knew what they saw: an ugly, upsetting scene between the two people they loved the most.

How much better for the kids—and me—if I could have just stayed in the house, pulled myself together, and hugged them to death when they came through the door. I could have called their dad later, out of earshot of the little ones. And although I could never give Billy his dream of having all of us as one big happy family again, I could have let him hold onto it a little longer while he worked out his life as a child of divorce. It was a security blanket of sorts for him, one that he would discard later when he didn't need it. Ripping it away from him like I did only hurt him—and for what purpose?

None of us are perfect, and when emotions run high, we tend to move even further away from that standard. That's why rules are so important. Impose a strict code of conduct on yourself to prevent hurting your kids unnecessarily. On top of that list put: never call their dad names—not to them, not in front of them, not to family or friends or anyone who might repeat it to them. Don't yell at him, don't fight with him, and don't say anything harsh about him. If you keep in mind how much they love him, you will put their dad off limits to all badmouthing and work out your differences with him away from them.

#4: Tell the Kids Good Things about Their Dad

Once you have mastered the "no bad-mouthing" rule, take it to the next step. Tell the kids good things about their dad. If I can do it, you can. And it produces such great results that it is a must for all moms, single or not.

I admit that initially this was tough for me. I had nothing good to say and was quite happy to keep it that way. But he was a key figure in my boys' lives, and they wanted to feel close to him. They no longer saw him every day, so the need was even greater. Why not give them greater insight into who he was and more knowledge of all he'd done? It would build their respect for him and make them even prouder to call him "Dad."

And who better than me to tell them about their dad—I knew the good. And where else would a five-year-old learn his father was handsome and smart, that he was a first-class attorney and a great athlete? So I began to tell them stories about their dad as a kid and about the funny things he had done over the years. And when I did, their faces would light up—they loved it. And I would often hear them repeating these stories to their friends.

I don't want you to think I was singing his praises by day and holding seminars on his finer qualities by night. I did it only when something triggered a good memory or when I heard one of my boys talking about him. Then I would add a positive comment about this man they loved.

I would also encourage them to talk about him openly. For instance, when the kids returned from a visit with their dad, I would ask them all about it. They were excited to talk, and I listened as they did. Sometimes the information wasn't all that welcomed—how much they liked his new girlfriend never settled too well. But I would keep the caustic comments to myself and allow the boys free rein over the conversation. I wanted them to feel comfortable talking about their dad in their own home, which meant no editorial comments from Mom.

Kids need to love their dad freely. When you build him up by telling your kids about his talents and accomplishments, you send them a powerfully important message: that it is okay for them to love him, that they have your consent, and that they can do so openly at home and in your presence. Then encourage them to do so. Remember, it's all about being a good mom.

#5: Let the Kids See Their Dad—as Often as Possible

When a dad lives in their home, kids grow close to him naturally. He is the man in their family, the one who hugs and squeezes them, checks their homework, drives them to school, or teaches them sports. He's in their daily life where he belongs, and the bond deepens with each passing day. This kind of home lends tremendous order to the lives of kids and provides them with a deep sense of belonging and security.

When divorce hits, the physical and emotional upheaval for kids is huge and can lead to thoughts of abandonment and low self-esteem. If these feelings are allowed to take root, serious problems will follow. The most effective way to keep this damage to a minimum is for both parents to be heavily involved in the lives of their kids. That means mom *and* dad.

In an editorial in the *Washington Post* on October 18, 2009, Patrick Welsh, an English teacher at T. C. Williams High School in Alexandria, Virginia, shed a bright light on the impact a dad can have on his children. Here is what he wrote:

"Why don't you guys study like the kids from Africa?"

In a moment of exasperation last spring, I asked that question to a virtually all-black class of 12th-graders who had done horribly on a test I had just given. A kid who seldom came to class—and was constantly distracting other students when he did—shot back: "It's because they have fathers who kick their butts and make them study."

Another student angrily challenged me: "You ask the class, just ask how many of us have our fathers living with us." When I did, not one hand went up.

I was stunned. These are good kids; I had grown attached to them over the school year. It hit me that these students, at T. C. Williams High School in Alexandria, understood what I knew all too well: The lack of a father in their lives had undermined their education.

My students knew intuitively that the reason they were lagging academically had nothing to do with race. And it wasn't because the school system had failed them. They knew that excuses about a lack of resources and access just didn't wash at the new, state-of-the-art, $100 million T. C. Williams, where every student is given a laptop and where there is open enrollment in Advanced Placement and honors courses. Rather, it was because their parents just weren't there for them—at least not in the same way that parents of kids who were doing well tended to be.*

Mr. Welch went on to tell of a senior in his Advanced Placement English class who gave his father the credit for his own academic accomplishments:

"He has always been on me; it's been hard to get away with much," the student said. He also told me that hardly any of his friends have their fathers living with them. "Their mothers are soft on them, and they don't get any push from home."

---

*Patrick Welsh, "Making the Grade Isn't About Race. It's About Parents," *Washington Post*, October 18, 2009, B1–2.

There are thousands of stories just like this one—all making the same point: involved dads make an enormous difference in the lives of their children. For the sake of their kids, single moms need to encourage this relationship whenever and however possible. A good dad is a priceless blessing. But it requires time spent together.

You can't make their dad be a good dad, but you can sure open the door to it. You can treat as sacred the court-appointed time for visitation. And if he can't make one of the designated days—no matter how weak the excuse—you can encourage another day. If he wants to see them even more, you can work with him to see that it happens. If he's late paying child support—or not paying at all—you still need to let him see the kids. It makes life tough on you—and you need to take whatever legal action necessary to get him to pay—but the kids need their dad. Their time with him belongs to them, and you should never take it from them so you can teach him a lesson.

There are lots of reasons dads don't see their kids, and single moms can't always make it happen. But when you consider how special this time is to your kids, you have to do whatever you can to give them as much of it as possible.

My son Billy brings this point home perfectly:

Mom had custody of us, Dad took us on the weekends, although he was a very busy attorney who traveled frequently to Riverside, and those trips sometimes spilled over into the weekends, limiting even that small amount of time with him. I always wished I could see him more often. I was very close to him, and being with him, spending any amount of time with him, made me feel like a million dollars.

The converse was also true: I always felt like something was missing when Dad wasn't around. Mom was great—she more than made up for the fact that we were essentially being raised by one parent. Dad didn't raise us; this wasn't his fault—it's not like he didn't try. But child custody arrangements, as they were (and granted, he agreed to the arrangements), prevented him from having any lasting impact on us. My brothers and I truly were products of our mother.

Those empty feelings were made even worse during the times Mom took us with her on her campaign trips. These occurred three times: once in Virginia for a month or two; once in Maryland, which lasted a whole third-grade semester; and finally a permanent move back to Virginia when I was ten. Dad did his best—he visited us occasionally at each place, which was a sacrifice given he was a named partner at a small Orange County law firm. It was great seeing him every time, but watching him leave was such heartbreak. Today I would trade most anything for a moment longer with Dad.

Unfortunately Billy is right; my kids did not have enough time with their dad. And though his death certainly contributed to this, it was a long way from being the only reason.

As critical as it is for kids to spend a goodly amount of quality time with both parents, divorce sometimes forces one parent or the other to take steps that make this kind of valuable arrangement nearly impossible. I know this better than anyone. It happened to me—as Billy said, on three separate occasions, the last of which moved the boys three thousand miles away from their dad.

It was on a June evening in 1987 that Bill left our California home. I had no job and no prospects of one. My past experience was political campaigns, and I had picked up a few since leaving the Treasury—but those were all temporary, which was exactly what I wanted at the time. They offered me a quick infusion of cash for the household, gave me great flexibility, and usually lasted no more than six months. This wasn't going to work anymore.

My ex agreed to send me money to pay bills until after the baby was born. (And he kept his word.) But his salary wasn't going to keep two households afloat for long. I needed to find permanent full-time employment but didn't know where to look considering I was three months pregnant and my best contacts were on the East Coast.

Then a truly amazing thing happened. A few weeks after Bill left I was asked to attend a private meeting with a potential presidential candidate. He was putting together his national campaign organization and asked if I would be his treasurer—basically the chief financial officer. It was a job I had done many times before, so there'd be no learning curve—and with the right staff I could do it by day and be home for dinner with the kids. The problem was that it meant I'd have to move to Washington for what I expected would be six months or so.

To be honest, I had no choice. I didn't have any other offers, the pay was good, and the job would carry me past my delivery date, or so I thought. What's more, Washington was my hometown, so the boys and I would be near my family. I accepted the position and a month later flew with my kids to Virginia.

One evening, about ten days after I had us comfortably situated in a small rental home in Arlington, Virginia, the candidate called. He couldn't go forward, he informed me; he couldn't bring himself to do what his political advisers said was necessary. They were adamant that he go negative against his opponents, but the other candidates were friends of his and he wouldn't say anything against them. He had gone into seclusion over the Labor Day weekend and there made the decision. He would withdraw from the race the next day and wanted me to be one of the first to know.

This man was a good friend and an even better person. He felt terrible for having dragged me and the boys across the country. But I understood; these things happened in the business of politics. I asked if he would keep me on for some of the cleanup work, and he agreed. That gave me another six weeks of employment. *Better than nothing,* I thought.

I had told no one about the impending divorce. But I needed to find a good divorce lawyer in California, so one night during this Virginia adventure of mine I confided in my youngest brother, Tom, and his wife, Theresa. They were both attorneys. Theresa strongly recommended I stay in Virginia. "Settle here," she advised, "where you have great employment opportunities. You need to think about how you're going to take care of your kids." She explained, "If you return to California and get a divorce there, the courts won't allow you to take the kids out of that state and away from their dad, no matter how good a job offer you get in Washington. You'll have no problem finding work here," she stressed, "but to take advantage of that you have to file for divorce here in Virginia."

Theresa made good sense and was looking out for me, but I couldn't think about raising the boys so far away from their dad. It wasn't fair to them, not if I could find a way to make a living in California. They were too young and needed to spend time with him, to see him often so they could grow close to him. I had to give their father a chance to be their dad.

For the boys' sake I returned to California after two months. Within days of this arrival I responded to an early morning knock on my front door and was promptly served with divorce papers. And that was that.

After Stuart was born I began to dig my way out of the nightmare of divorce and into the dream of a good life as the single mom. A pattern soon developed: Wednesday nights and every other weekend the boys spent with their dad.

The first few years Stuart didn't join them. Their dad would entertain the kids at playgrounds, pools, arcades, and, of course, at Disneyland, which was only twenty minutes up the road. Quality time with the oldest, their dad explained, meant the infant had to stay home. I wholeheartedly agreed. After all, Stuart was my "Babe," and I wanted him near, as any mama bear would.

Then there were Sundays. Their dad had every other weekend, but he wanted the boys to go to church with me so he would drop them off early Sunday morning. Again I agreed; this would be best for the kids.

It wasn't long after these adjustments were made that their dad began to find the remaining court-appointed times too restrictive. He began to treat them more like suggestions, explaining he needed more flexibility. He would call and change the Wednesday visit to Thursday or the Friday night pick-up to Saturday morning, often with only a few hours' notice.

This drove me crazy; I couldn't make my own plans. Instead I found myself waiting for the call, and when it came, I would agree to the alternative time, hang up, and be furious. I could have told him "no," but the kids wanted to see him, and why else was I in California?

I had to get control—I couldn't let him have so much influence over my moods. And I knew he wasn't going to change, so I had to. I decided never to make plans for the chunks of time he was scheduled to have the kids. Then I wouldn't be inconvenienced if he called to tell me about his latest conflict. He'd just be giving me more time to be with my boys. As a working mom I never felt I saw them enough, so this worked perfectly. I no longer cared when he saw the boys as long as he saw them.

But this wasn't the case for Billy, who knew one weekday from another and would wait all week for Wednesday because that's when he would see his dad. He would count the days and be so excited when it finally came. But more and more often I would have to tell him that his dad called and changed his visit to another time. Billy would get so upset, which quickly turned to anger. "But Dad promised me," he'd yell. "He promised me." It was heartbreaking.

Time with their dad took another hit when their dad remarried. Unfortunately the boys did not feel comfortable overnighting in his new home. They would call me in the middle of the night, crying and begging me to come and get them. It didn't take long before weekend visitation was reduced to Saturday. But the boys still looked forward to it.

Five years after their dad left, with a court agreement in hand, my kids and I took a six-month leave of absence from California when my brother Pat decided to challenge the first President Bush in the 1992 Republican primary. He asked me to run his campaign. I couldn't think of a more exciting challenge and wanted to be there for him. The boys and I moved to Maryland, renting a home close to my mom, who was finding living alone tough going. When Billy and Tommy left for school, I had my nanny take Stuart and go to Granny's to fix her lunch, clean her house, and drive her anywhere she wanted to go. On weekends the boys and I would often head to Granny's. She loved the company and needed it desperately. Being back east felt so right for so many reasons. When we returned to California six months later, I began to think of moving there permanently.

Here is how I looked at it. I lived in California so the kids would know their dad. I gave it my best for six years. I didn't owe their dad a day, but I owed my kids every one of them. But their dad was not doing my kids justice, and the boys were getting to the age when they were becoming aware of this. I didn't want them hurt any more—and his cavalier approach to their visits was doing just that.

At the same time the East was drawing me back—both personally and professionally. There were family and cousins for the kids, and there was my mom. I wanted her to live with us, to be surrounded by family in her final years, and I wanted my kids to have a chance to know their only living grandparent.

Then there was the political world. My brother would run again, the work would be steady, the pay would be good, and the hours would be flexible. I could drive the kids to school, see their recitals and games, and stay with them if they were sick. And yes, I admit, I wanted to be part of my brother's campaign. I had paid for their dad's visits east before and I would do so again.

I would have liked to have given the boys more time with their dad, to have lived in California longer, but the advantages of moving east were great for my family, and their dad wasn't giving me much of a reason to stay.

I went to court to request permission to move my family permanently away from California. The judge looked at the irregularity of Bill's visits with his sons and sent me on my way with his legal blessing. My boys and I moved to Virginia, and their dad came east to see them every few months. After a few years the boys asked their dad if they could also spend time with him during the summer. He agreed, and rather than have all three of them descend on him at the same time, he took one at a time and vacationed with him for a solid week. The kids loved every minute of this private time with their dad. This arrangement was far from perfect, and I knew it. But as a single parent I had to make the tough decisions when it came to what was best for my family.

That's what single moms have to do—give their kids a chance to see and know their dad, then hope he does right by them. There is no question it's best for the kids when he is extremely involved in their lives. But it isn't always possible, and when it is, it doesn't always happen. The key to remember is he doesn't have to live up to your high standards (or mine) to give his kids an important and meaningful relationship; he just needs to be in their lives enough so they can have a dad to love. If you doubt this, just recall what my son Stuart wrote about the time he had with his Disneyland dad: "What little time I did spend with him is more precious to me than all the riches in the world, more precious than anything, save time spent with my Mom."

Compensate for No Dad in the Home

In November of 2010 the Associated Press reported that "seventy-two percent of black babies are born to unmarried mothers"* That's whole communities of kids with no dad in their home, none in their lives, none in the homes or lives of their relatives or friends. Unless a coach, a teacher, or some other strong, positive male role model happens to enter their world, these kids will not know what a two-parent family even looks like—and will have no way to learn. Devastating statistics tell the rest of that story.

You can't let that happen to your kids. Not only must single moms give their kids a fighting chance at some kind of relationship with their dad; they also have to compensate for not having him in their home. Kids need to learn firsthand what a good father means to a family; they need to have time to observe how he leads his children by guidance

---

*Jesse Washington, "Blacks Struggle with 72 percent Unwed Mother Rate," MSNBC, November 7, 2010, http://www.msnbc.msn.com/id/39993685/ns/health -womens_health/t/blacks-struggle-percent-unwed-mothers-rate/.

and example. How else will they learn what a family with a father is like and how good it is? And without this knowledge, how can you expect them to want it for themselves and their kids? How will your boys learn what it means to be a good husband and a great dad? How will your girls learn the traits to look for in a potential husband and the father of their children? You must find other ways for your kids to learn these critical lessons.

My second son, Tommy, addressed this topic:

Growing up without a dad around was tough. Though I loved my childhood and wouldn't change anything about it (well maybe a few less-than-productive choices in high school), I am reluctant to say it was not the ideal upbringing for children.

A strong male presence in the home is an irreplaceable blessing. A father figure provides a solid foundation for his children's up-bringing. And in my case, my father would have taught me many invaluable lessons that nobody else could have—lessons that I yearned for while growing up.

One such lesson, which most kids my age learned in their earlier years, is how a man should treat a woman. I am the kid who was pushing girls over logs in kindergarten and chasing them with a stick if they dared come near me. Had I been exposed to a loving husband showing acts of kindness toward his wife, I might have learned to deal with girls differently. If I had a dad in my home during high school, I believe I would have shown greater respect to the girls I dated or with whom I hung out. I truly believe that the most important thing a father can do for his kids is show them how much he loves their mother.

Another problem of a fatherless home is that new, unconventional, authoritative types enter their lives. In my case, it was au pairs and nannies. I was fortunate to have a fantastic nanny for the beginning of my childhood. But when she married and moved on with her life, I was left with a sense of distrust toward anyone in authority who didn't carry the sacred title of "Mom." She was the queen, the president, and the empress of my world, and anyone who tried to play that role, in my mind, was committing the equivalent of a familial coup d'état—and it was my responsibility to stop it. These feelings of animosity played a significant role in the resignation or firing of four out of the five au pairs that stepped into the Buchanan Republic. With a father at home, I might have better understood my role as a child and their role as a caretaker.

Kids need parents for a lot more than food, shelter, and a trip to the park. Their mom and dad are the anchors of their life, the cornerstones of their family. It is within this unit that kids are meant to learn the lessons of life.

It is equally important that your kids feel at ease in families with a dad, that they are not nervous or apprehensive about a strong male presence. An emotionally healthy development depends on this.

To compensate for a fatherless home, find good male role models and make them part of your kids' lives. Look for solid men and strong fathers among family members, friends, coaches, teachers, church leaders, camp counselors, and scout leaders. They are there. It is your job to identify them and create the opportunity for these men to have an impact on your children.

Extended family, single-sex schools, and church are where I found amazing people who willingly entered my kids' lives and provided remarkable examples for them.

My younger brother Brian (nicknamed Buck) is a doctor in Bedford, Virginia, which is less than four hours from our home. He and his wife have five kids about the same age as mine, and the path between our two homes was well traveled. They are a great family, and Buck was a superb example of a dad for my boys. I made certain our families were close.

Buck's youngest son, Anton, and my son Stuart were best of friends and as tight as brothers. They visited one another several times a year. On one trip to our designated pick-up/drop-off point—a bookstore in Charlottesville—Stuart said to me, "Mom, I love going to Uncle Buck's. It feels so much like home." The words warmed my heart.

I was raised with seven brothers and a strong dad. It was a rough-and-tumble environment, and I didn't want my sons to fear it. My boys were surrounded by women—a nanny, me, and, for several years, my mother. Although I was as tough as most men, they didn't know this. They needed to feel comfortable and confident in the world of men—not just women—so I looked for ways to make that happen.

When I came across a single-sex elementary school, beginning in third grade, I jumped at it. All the teachers at The Heights School were male; they focused on the three "R's" and the classics, and, most importantly, they let boys be boys. Every day my kids worked out life with some of the finest men you could meet.

Then, following in the steps of their grandfather, all seven uncles, and most of their male cousins, the boys attended Gonzaga College High School, an all-male Jesuit school in the center of Washington, DC. Again their daily lives were packed with terrific male teachers and coaches.

My church was another great source of support to my family. When teenage boys tell you how much they love their church leaders, you know something mighty good is happening. The powerfully positive influence these inspired men had on my boys was beyond extraordinary.

I was determined that, as youngsters and teenagers, my boys would learn what it meant to be good men, loyal husbands, and committed fathers. Girls need the same lessons in their life. If you want your kids to aspire to be good spouses and great parents, you have to show them what it means and how it's done. You have to find examples of these and make them part of your kids' lives.

The Bottom Line

Although it is best to have Dad in their homes, the next best thing is for children to have Dad in their lives. Allowing kids to maintain and develop a close relationship with their father is unequivocally one of the most important things a single mom can do for her kids.

So here's Rule #2: "Let their dad be their dad." Never bad-mouth him. Do nothing that would make your kids think or feel poorly about him. Let them see their dad as often as possible, and tell them good things about him so they can love him openly in their own home.

This rule applies equally to all parents whether they're single or not. What greater gift can a dad give his kids than to honor their mother—and tell them how amazing she is? Creating a sense of love and respect for one another in the home is at the heart of good parenting.

But if you're a single mom you have the added responsibility of the Ancillary to Rule #2: "Compensate for the lack of a dad in the home." The evidence is overwhelming that children raised with a dad in their home are more likely to thrive than are those without. Clearly there are lessons learned in that environment that aren't available outside it. If you are raising a child alone, find good two-parent families and make them a part of your kids' world. Let your kids learn through family and friends the critical and unique lessons taught by observing a good man being a husband and a father. And it is up to you single dads to make certain your kids understand and appreciate the important role of wife and mother.

Chapter Three

Put the Kids First

I turned one of the bedrooms in my California home into an office and worked there whenever possible. One day while I was on the phone with a candidate, two-year-old Tommy came on in without a stitch of clothing and tried desperately to get my attention. I kept mouthing to him "one minute" and used my index finger to reinforce the message.

My delay tactic went on way too long for this kid. So he stepped on top of my briefcase, which was flat on the floor, and peed all over it. *An effective means of communicating*, I thought, *for a nonverbal toddler*. Without saying a word he let me know what he thought about my work *and* got what he wanted—my full attention. I killed the call (no, not the kid), cleaned up the mess, and went off with the winner of this particular exchange.

The traditional two-parent family provides children a tight, secure environment that gives them a powerful sense of belonging. They are loved, guided, and nurtured within its walls. When a divorce occurs, this protective structure—which the kids desperately need—takes a terrible blow, and they fear it won't survive. They become anxious about what will happen to them. As a single parent, only you can guarantee that your kids will always feel that they're part of a great family—a feeling that will allow them to develop and thrive as if they still had both parents at home. But the only way this will ever happen is if you are totally committed to them.

Here's the bottom line: your kids need you—your time, your energy, your heart, your guidance, your understanding, your discipline. They need all of you. Just being nearby doesn't cut it. They have to know they belong to you, that they are the center of your world. They need to be able to lean on you for strength, to feel secure and unafraid because you are their mom and will never let them down. That kind of trust doesn't come easy. It requires constant sacrifice. There is no other way. If you are committed to doing everything for your kids—if you are determined to give them a chance to beat the odds—then you have to put your kids first in your life.

This doesn't mean sometimes or most of the time; it means all the time. Your life has to revolve around your children. Your decisions need to be based on what is best for them. Being a great mom has to be your primary goal in life; your kids have a right to expect this, and you have an obligation to give it to them.

Often, when moms have their first child, they'll tell you that this baby is the most important thing in their lives. I said the same. But "always putting my kids first" took on new meaning when I became a single mom. I had no idea how difficult it would be. But it didn't take long to figure out—and the sacrifice changed my life forever.

Find Time to Be with Your Kids

For years I'd hear so-called experts talk about the need for moms to set aside personal time and private space that's all their own. And every time I did, I laughed out loud. What were these people talking about? I'd wonder. Did they know anything about being a mom, much less a single mom? When my boys were toddlers, I was lucky to make it through a shower without one of them coming in looking for me. And for years I'd set Stuart up with a little play area right next to the toilet. Hey, it was for his own good—no telling what damage his brothers could do to him if I were out of earshot of his screams.

As for space—there wasn't a square inch of our home they didn't claim. One summer Stuart commandeered my bedroom as a military airfield for his scores of small metal fighting planes. On one of my nocturnal trips to the bathroom I stepped on a wing tail. A number of stitches and a tetanus shot later, I made a case for a landing strip between the bed and bathroom.

You might ask, why didn't I have him use his own room to play? Well, first of all, it wasn't available—a half-million Lego pieces occupied that space. More importantly, Stuart wasn't there to play with me (he knew my knowledge of the topic was limited to the plane I stepped on); he just wanted to be near me. And so he was.

Around this same time I put a television in my bedroom in hopes of occasionally sneaking in a few chick flicks—my feeble attempt at creating "time for me." I must have lost my mind. Did I really think the boys would watch their show in the den while I, blissfully alone in my bedroom, watched a tearjerker? It was never going to happen. Those boys were in search of me by the first commercial and wasted no time joining me. "Movies in Mom's room" became their new adventure, and they insisted "rule of the house" apply—the family chose the program or movie, not its senior member.

I knew popcorn was going to be the next thing to join me in my bed. So, before things got totally out of hand, I moved the television into the furnace room and gave up all hope of ever seeing *Pride and Prejudice* again until the boys left home.

Although there is nothing wrong with having a little time to yourself, the kids had it right. As a working parent I didn't see them enough as it was. I was at the office all day, and when I came home, I cooked dinner, cleaned dishes, checked homework, and did whatever was needed to prepare for the next day. What's more, there was no dad to be with them when I was busy. So when I did find—or make—time to relax, they had every right to it. At least that's how I saw it.

You and your kids are in this world as a family, not as a group of individuals, so live that way. Do everything you can together—even if you hate Harry Potter (which would be a perfectly reasonable position), watch the movie with them anyway. Look for ways to be with your kids. Getting bogged down in the housework is easy, but the dishes don't need to be washed before the kids are in bed—spend that extra fifteen minutes playing, reading, or talking to them. If the kids are old enough pick a classic, then read them a chapter a night. Set aside time not for yourself but for the kids—how else will they learn that they belong to you and you to them?

When my boys were little, we did everything together, from grocery shopping to Saturday night movies. But I also knew it was important to have "private time," as we called it, with each one of them. So when Billy began kindergarten at a school thirty-five minutes from our home, I knew a gift had been dropped in my lap.

Tommy wouldn't follow his older brother for another couple years, so I was looking at more than a half-hour alone with Billy nearly every weekday morning—for two solid years. I was thrilled with this development and determined not to waste this precious time with my oldest. I soon realized, however, that although Billy was precocious, a daily thirty-minute discussion with a six-year-old didn't come easy, especially when you knew nothing about Nintendo. I would have to be creative.

I decided that if there wasn't a poem to practice, a spelling lesson to review, or some other pressing issue to work through, then I'd have him choose an article from the front page of the Los Angeles Times. I'd have him read the headline and the first few paragraphs out loud (which would improve his reading skills and his vocabulary), and then we'd talk about it (which would give him knowledge of current events). I considered it a brilliant plan—terrific private time for my son and me—and educational to boot. At least that's how I saw it until I got a call to come see the headmaster.

It came the same day that Billy had been drawn to a story on the death penalty. He read it and we talked about it at great length. In hindsight the kid did have a lot more questions than usual. I told him what was involved and discussed the pros and cons—undoubtedly with an emphasis on the pros.

What I later learned was that Billy had found an almost immediate use for his newly acquired knowledge. There were a few kids at school who regularly picked on him. Fully armed with the facts, he approached them on the playground and threatened them with capital punishment, explaining in detail the different methods that could be used. The scared little bullies ratted him out.

Although I was mighty impressed at how well Billy took to his morning lesson, I was going to have to be more circumspect when it came to topics we choose—or I was going to get Billy tossed out of school.

Strong families don't just happen—they take time, effort, and sacrifice. There has to be a routine established—one that includes your active participation. Your kids need to know you are part of their everyday life, so you have to eat with them, talk to them about their day, help them with their homework, and read to them or watch a favorite TV show before bed. Again, kids need to be put ahead of the dishes, the cleaning, the Internet, and your job. It's called family life—and you are central to it.

Once you commit to putting your kids first in your life, everything else falls into place. Your space is their space and your free time belongs to them. You are a family, and your kids see it and feel it every day. They learn to expect it—and see themselves as part of this larger unit. And they relax knowing this is how it will be for the rest of their lives. This is the only way to give your kids a true sense of family—and you have to sacrifice mightily to make it happen. Even then it doesn't mean there won't be problems—but it does mean your kids will have a fighting chance to beat the odds against children of single moms. And that's your job.

Let's talk frankly about some of the sacrifices you need to make— and remember, not only can you do it, you *must* do it.

Put Your Kids Ahead of Your Work

With few exceptions, single parents have to work. But your job has to accomplish two things: it has to pay you enough to take care of your kids *and* it has to be flexible enough so you can be there for them. If it doesn't do both, you have to start planning on how you're going to get one that does. Then find one. You have no choice—providing for your kids, but not seeing them, doesn't work.

Over the years I've heard much about the supermom—the woman who has it all—family, career, success. Don't believe this for a minute— she doesn't exist. And as a mom you already have the best of the lot anyway—the kids. Don't risk losing them while you are trying to have it all. Your career can be put on hold—your kids cannot.

This is a particularly difficult issue for many. It puts them face to face with a choice between what's best for them and what's best for their family. Although working moms everywhere have changed positions so they could be home with their kids in the evenings and on weekends, too many who could do this have not.

Many professional women argue that they've worked too hard getting to where they are, that they've got too much to lose if they put it all on hold, that they've grown accustomed to the money their career provides. I suspect many are just scared. It's a huge change for them, a significant sacrifice that takes them out of their secure world and drops them into unchartered waters. But being a good mom means putting your kids ahead of your career along with everything else in your life. And there are lots of good ways to do it.

An attorney friend loved her work in a law firm, but after her son was born she stopped putting in the long hours. She wanted to see her baby before he went to sleep at night. But her partners kept pressuring her to get her billable hours back up. She became anxious at home and at the office—feeling she wasn't doing a good job anywhere. She decided to get out of the rat race and became a public prosecutor—government hours, sick leave, and no overtime required. Her peace of mind more than compensated for the pay cut, and today she is a judge.

Another friend, a pediatrician, gave up her practice when she had children, opting instead to work part time at a hospital emergency room. She sacrificed the money and prestige for more time with her kids, all the while staying involved in her profession.

Soon after I became a mom a friend in the White House contacted me and asked if I would allow him to recommend me for a Cabinet post—a minor one, I'm sure, but nonetheless an attractive possibility. I told him no. The position would never allow me to be the kind of mom I wanted to be. I chose instead to work part time. When I became a single parent I choose to start my own business rather than pursue a corporate position. It was the only way I could be certain I'd have control over my work hours.

Later, when the boys were in elementary school, a media executive offered me a position as cohost of the political talk show *Equal Time*. The money was amazing, but the program was live at 7:30 p.m. That meant I'd need to be in studio from 4 p.m. to 7:30 p.m.—and would get home about 8:30 p.m. every night of the week. I turned it down. If I did this for two years, I told the executive, my kids would be running drugs by the time they were in high school. And I meant it.

He called back and asked, "How about a 6 p.m. taping?" Again I said no—still too risky. I thought I had lost the job, but they called a third time and offered to tape the show at 4:30 p.m. That's when I said yes. They made it work for me—but if they hadn't, I would never have looked back. I needed to be home at night, and nothing was going to interfere with that.

The key for every working parent is to be honest with yourself— does your work conflict with your ability to be a good parent? Is there another position, either closer to home or more family friendly, that you should consider until your kids are older? Can you cut your living expenses—move to a smaller home or an apartment, trade in the fancy car for a cheaper used one, take cheaper vacations—so you can afford a less demanding position? Remember: the greatest thing you can give your kids is your time—to be there for them at every turn in their lives.

If your job in any way conflicts with your responsibility to be a good mom, you need to search out other options, find out what else is available. Be determined in your efforts to find a family-friendly environment in which to work. They are there, but it's up to you to make it happen. Single moms are a quality bunch—we are hard-working, reliable, and often overqualified. And because we have kids depending on us, we are focused—and employers know it. There are emerging businesses that specialize in finding part-time and flexible-time employment for working moms. This might work for you, or it might not. But you have to look and you have to ask. And for your kids' sake, you have to be willing to sacrifice.

Unfortunately not everyone has options. Take, for instance, single moms without marketable skills. Often their jobs don't pay enough, lack security, or demand long hours—or a combination of the above. These moms immediately need to establish a plan to improve their situation by learning a business or gaining a skill. There are opportunities available—a nearby trade school or community college, a training position with a local business, or a stint in the military. It may mean that for a few years you'll need to rely on family or friends to help with the kids more heavily than you'd like. It may mean two nights a week of school and studying every night after the kids are asleep. Or it could require a second job while you're in training.

These additional demands on your time won't be easy, but you have no choice. You have to get yourself in a position to be able to provide for your kids *and* be there for them. Hopefully someone close to you can help so the kids don't feel your absence as much. But it's only temporary, and you're doing it so you can be the kind of mom they need. Remember: it's what we do for our children that make them understand how much we love them.

Single parents have an obligation to find a way to care for their kids and to always be there for them. Dogged determination can open up new avenues of possibilities, but you have to start searching for what will work for you, then throw yourself into getting it. And you can't quit until you've succeeded. Your kids are counting on you.

Being a parent has to be your first job. The second one, the one that pays, is essential, but it should never become more important to you than time with your children. Kids are guided through life by your example far more than your words. So show them how much they mean to you by making them first in all aspects of your life. It won't work any other way.

Don't Expect Smooth—and Ask for Help When It Gets Rough

As a self-employed mom I learned that it was best to have several sources of income. That way when one fell through—and they always did—my boys still ate. So when my television and political work led to occasional paid speeches, I was thrilled. They paid well and usually involved no more than twenty-four hours away from home. For the most part the kids were fine with these short trips. If they had a paper due the next day, they would e-mail me their draft, and I would edit it after the speech and send it back. When they woke up the next morning, they would print off the final product and be on their way to school.

When Stuart grew older, however, he began to face some difficulties in his life and needed me near. Often I'd take him with me when I traveled, but this wasn't always possible, and some days it was a struggle for us both.

When Stuart was nine, for instance, I agreed to a debate in Texas. It came with a sizable fee, and I could fly in and out the same day. *Sweet*, I thought, *the kids would hardly miss me*. The only twist was the topic—the impact of U.S. trade policy on farmers and related agribusiness. Trade policy was one of my passions, but I knew nothing about pigs and beef. I barely even ate them. To make matters worse, my opponent was going be a respected economist. Serious prep time was required.

The night before the speech I surrounded myself with research material and was deep into it when Stuart joined me. He was really sick. The next several hours he did nothing but moan and vomit. I was distraught.

It was his third such episode in as many months. On the other two occasions I had checked for appendicitis but found no sign of it. It made no sense to me, but because he was always better in the morning, I wrote it off as the twelve-hour flu. (Does such a thing even exist?)

But this time Stuart had picked the one night that I really needed sleep. I couldn't debate the economist with no sleep and no preparation, and if Stuart was better in the morning, I couldn't cancel (needed the money too badly). Overwhelmed and exhausted, I began to demand Stuart feel relief after he threw up. Everyone felt better when they threw up, I told him, so he needed to do the same. (I am always amazed at how totally irrational I could sometimes be.)

There was no improvement in his condition when the clock struck 4 A.M. But I made him go to his own room anyhow. I had to get at least a few hours of sleep. When I woke, I found the poor kid sprawled out on the floor outside my bedroom door. I felt awful! I had sent this poor little kid away to be alone with all his illness so I could get a cat nap.

Once I determined he was better, I put him in my bed and headed for the airport. On the layover in Atlanta I placed an SOS call to my friend Pat Choate, an economist who had been raised on a farm. What luck! He gave me a crash course on the economy of agriculture. On the final leg of the trip I put together my opening remarks and was ready for action when my car pulled up in front of the convention hall.

That day was all about survival: no need to excel—just get through it standing. With this minimum standard accomplished I returned home to pamper Stuart. Then it was all about guilt—something else that plagues us moms way too often.

A month later Stuart had another such episode. This time I had learned my lesson. I took the kid straight to the emergency room, certain he had appendicitis. When his surgeon said it wasn't, I refused to leave. I knew better.

Stuart's personal doctor did additional tests and found that my diagnosis was right. The surgeon returned and removed the cause of Stuart's painful, fitful nights.

(When I told this story to my sister, a terrific parent, she made me feel a tiny bit better. One night her son, a college freshman home for Christmas, woke her in the middle of the night complaining of terrible stomach pain. She told him his pajamas were probably too tight and to put on looser ones. She then turned over and went back to sleep. Later that night he returned bent over in pain and told her she needed to take him to the hospital. He had a kidney stone. Sometimes even the best of us don't get it right!)

Being a working mom is never smooth. Even with all your efforts, life is still going to get complicated. Remember, two-parent families have two adults that can be called into action. As a single parent, the responsibility is often all yours, and no matter how hard you try, there're going to be times when your work and your kids' needs conflict, even with a family-friendly work environment.

To survive the tough times you need to have a kind of support system of your own. Identify relatives or friends who are willing to step in to help if all else fails, individuals with whom the kids are comfortable and whom you can trust to care for them properly.

At first I didn't want to ask anyone for help. Pride, I suppose. But that was foolish. I quickly learned to find friends who could watch my kids all day—or night, when necessary. When my boys joined teams, I was like a scout at their first few games—in search of parents who could help me get my kids to and from practices. I found so many people ready to assist at every stage of my boys' young lives. But this doesn't happen unless you do the groundwork. I couldn't do it alone. So for the sake of my kids, I did what didn't come naturally to this lady: I asked for help. And it was always there when I needed it.

Put Your Kids Ahead of Your Love Life

Herein lies the greatest sacrifice of all—and there is no way around it. Saying the kids were the center of my life was one thing, but could I live a life in which I *always* put them first? I had promised myself I would, but doing it proved far more difficult than I could've ever imagined.

After the divorce I occasionally toyed with the idea of meeting a wonderful man, someone who would love my kids like I did and be a great dad to them. I didn't worry with the details—just the big, glorious, happy-ever-after part. But it was in the details that the devil was lurking. I know because I met such a guy.

He was fun, kind, and great company. We dated casually for several months and I liked him—I liked him a lot. We would usually go out when the big boys were with their father, but even then, it was tough to justify. Stuart was still a baby and didn't go to his dad's, so I would have to get a babysitter for him. That never felt right. Those evenings out could have been special time for my Babe and me, but instead I was off on a date.

What's more, this good man had a right to expect me to put aside quality time for him. But how was that going to happen? All my spare time needed to go to the kids—and there wasn't enough of it as it was.

Friday evening was movie night with the boys. Likewise, the weekend was pure family time, and I worked to make it special. With friends in tow, my boys and I would go biking or swimming. Or I'd take them to a local park or to the swap meet where they would buy army paraphernalia. Afterward they would watch their favorite TV show or put in a movie while I made milkshakes or smoothies and fed them homemade cookies or brownies for the afternoon snack. Their friends stayed for dinner and often for the night.

These were fun times for me; they were my boys' childhood. I realized I couldn't share this precious time with anyone else. It belonged to my kids—and I had to be there with them. What's more, I wanted to be.

As for dating when the boys were at their dad's—that was never going to work. Stuart didn't go to his dad's for the first eighteen months of his life, and after that he seldom went overnight. As time passed the older boys spent fewer and fewer Friday nights at their dad's, and eventually they were picked up Saturday morning and dropped off that night.

Then there was the problem of attachment. What if my boys grew close to the man I was dating and then, after six months or a year, we broke up? Another father figure come and gone—I couldn't let that happen. I wasn't going to put them through that ever again, not if I could prevent it, and this time I could.

And at least one of my boys was especially susceptible to becoming attached to father figures. A friend of mine took Tommy to Disneyland in his Jeep when he was about eight—just the two of them. For weeks this kid would look out the window hoping to see this new friend coming up the front steps to visit him. A few years later Tommy joined me on a campaign trip when his Uncle Pat was running for president. (I took each of the boys with me on at least one campaign trip.) While we were flying from one location to another, one of our secret service agents took Tommy aside and showed him his weapons—including the one carried in the proverbial violin case. He was kind, and Tommy couldn't get enough—throughout that trip he hung as close to this agent as he could in hopes of getting more attention.

How badly would he have been hurt if he had become attached to someone I was dating, someone he saw almost every weekend, who threw the ball around with him and raced him on bike trips? To then have this man walk out of our life would have been brutal for this kid. I couldn't risk it.

Then there was the awful scare that dating sent through my boys. I saw it up close when Billy was only seven years old and still dreaming his parents would one day get back together. His dad picked him up one evening and introduced him to the woman he was going to marry the following Saturday. The kid broke down when he got home. "Why," he kept asking me, "hadn't Dad given me time to get to know her? How could he marry someone I've never met? How," he cried, "could Dad do any of this without talking to me?"

There was great wisdom in this young boy, and I had no answers that would comfort him. He was scared and anxious, uncertain what it all meant for him. He worried about how it would impact his time with his dad, upset he'd have to share him with a woman he didn't even know. And he feared the same might happen with me.

To put his mind at rest I promised him I would never remarry without his approval. Unless his brothers and he liked the man and gave me the thumbs up, it would not happen. It was a promise I meant to keep—how else could I expect the kids to feel secure about their life? If we were to be a close-knit family—as I desperately wanted— then I had to give them a vote before introducing a new member to it.

It took only about a year of being home alone with my three boys for me to face the reality that, although I was a single mom, I was not single. I had to decide who was going to be first in my life, my kids or me. I chose the kids, broke off the relationship with this good man, and never looked back. (Well, maybe a few times).

And anyhow, those boys were never going to give me their approval to remarry. I was all theirs, and they were going to keep it that way. We all won.

Dating doesn't work for single moms for lots of reasons. It takes you away from your kids when they most need you—in the evenings and on the weekends. It unnerves them, unsettles them, giving them reason to believe that another major adjustment could befall them. And instead of sending them a steady message that constantly assures them that you'll always be there for them—something they desperately need—you're off making sweet talk with someone outside the family. You might as well tell your kids that you'll always be there for them— that is, if nothing better comes along.

But the most powerful argument has to be the risk it carries of deeply hurting your kids all over again. If they become attached to the new man in your life and one of you breaks it off, they will suffer terribly. You simply can't bring men in and out of their lives; you can't put your kids through that again and again. It isn't fair to them. And there is no amount of justification that's going to change that. The same holds true for single dads.

That being said, there are those occasions when girl meets guy and it works out well for everyone, including the kids. I have several friends for whom this was the case. They met their future husbands in the course of their lives—at work or at church—and were able to get to know him without impacting their time with their children. Then when they decided to take the relationship to a more serious level, they spent time together on evenings and weekends for only a few months—enough time to determine if they wanted to get married. After that, they included the kids in their time together and married within several months.

Sure, it could work—and does, in limited circumstances. The key is how many evenings and weekends are you going to spend away from those who need you most? If it starts to add up, your kids will pay the price. Make no mistake about it.

As a single mom the most important thing you can do is put your kids first every day and every night, and never let anyone or anything come between you and them. Dating does that. It risks hurting your children deeply. If, however, you take evenings and weekends and reserve them for family time, you'll never regret it. And neither will your kids. In short, dating is about what's best for you. Home with the kids is about what's best for them.

Plan Time Away with Your Kids

When I was first divorced, I had less than no money. But I was still determined to take my boys on vacations. I knew from my own experience that time away with parents was different than time at home. I saw them in a more relaxed environment, and we grew closer as a family.

I still remember when I was growing up biking all over Stone Harbor, New Jersey, with my brother Buck and playing Hearts with my brother Jack for hours at a time. And every year I loved to watch my dad swim lengths right beyond the waves. No one swam lengths in the ocean—no one but my dad. I wanted my boys to have these kinds of memories as well, and I wanted the closeness that comes from creating them.

To help assure that our vacations worked this way I established a few vacation rules: no friends, no electronic games, and no television. This forced the boys to talk and play with one another. It worked marvelously.

From the time they were toddlers we went away as a family every summer. And I have no doubt that these trips contributed enormously to the terrific relationships my boys have with one another today. I chose places I knew the kids would like, and when they were older, I would find a nearby historical site and, much to their chagrin, turn it into a day trip.

As I considered possible destinations for our family outings I was initially drawn to "boy things"—like camping, an exercise about which I had no interest or appreciation. But I did have boys, and camping fit perfectly into my budget that first summer as a single mom. Yosemite National Park offered a week's pass that included a campsite and parking for less than $100—and there was free bus transportation throughout the park. My nanny, who loved camping, agreed to join us. The Babe would sleep in the playpen inside the tent with the nanny and one of the big boys. The other son would sleep with me in the station wagon. The two boys could switch out— I would not.

All I could think about that first night was: here I am, the former Treasurer of the United States, sleeping in my car and calling it vacation. My nanny was adamant we do it right—every meal cooked over the campfire. After one day of that nonsense I was looking for a Plan B. She asked if I would mind if she spent a day hiking. Plan B was formed. I sent her on her way the next morning, and as soon as she was out of sight I gathered the kids from the dirt holes they were playing in and we took the bus to the stop next to the golden arches. We would upgrade for lunch and eat at the Pizza Hut and dinner would be at any one of the other fine dining establishments along the bus route. Life was looking up.

I always let the boys buy a little something to remind them of our vacation. That day they spotted ram horns—the kind you blow—and returned to the campsite with them. At dawn the next morning four-year-old Tommy was blowing up a storm as he walked all over the campsite. The awful noise woke me and a few others. I heard voices coming out of tents yelling, "Someone stop that [*bleepin'*] kid!" I let him go on awhile—no one was going to talk about my son that way without paying a price.

In late afternoon I would take the kids down to the stream near the camp on the pretense of hanging out on the small beach. Then when we got close, I would grab one of them and drag him into the water. It was so frigid they wouldn't go voluntarily, but it was the quickest way to get them clean. This soon turned into catch me if you can, and we were all laughing hysterically.

At night the kids and I sat around the fire making s'mores and playing games. Then the boys would collapse in their sleeping bags and I would walk a quarter of a mile to the hot showers. These are still precious memories for me—and they are tender. It was my first summer as a single mom, and out there in the woods I learned that we would make it—my boys and I—and we would have fun doing it.

Over the years we went to beaches and mountains, dude ranches and Disneyland. We ate at fast food dives and five-star restaurants. We went to battlefields and presidential homes. But most of all we had great fun being together. It was what I wanted for them, and they grew to expect it every summer—and these excursions provided my family with some of our finest memories. Stuart gives his account of one:

Floaties were my best friend back when I was eye level with the rest of the world's knees. I proudly sported the inflatable biceps whenever my family went to the pool. Or beach. Or sometimes just the mall. Okay, maybe not the mall, but you get the idea. I loved them.

I also loved following in my brothers' footsteps, and because they were older, bigger, and, thus, far more capable of satiating their adventurous spirits than I, oftentimes I was left to take baby steps while they were off sprinting.

A perfect example is the family outing to a water park when I was just a tiny little kid. Mom and I have always been best friends, so when it came to trips like this, we never had any problems sticking together while my two brothers ran off in search of certain doom.

On this particular occasion I had bravely left my floaties at home. Seeing my brothers run off toward the aptly named "Summit Plummet" waterslide, I started to work up the courage to get on my very first waterslide. Of course, watching my brothers free-fall off this skyscraper of a ride did not help my cause. As Mom and I walked around the park, I nibbled on my churro and eyed the seagulls suspiciously, all the while scanning the place for the perfect slide to start my daredevil career. There were several requirements it had to meet. Of course, it couldn't end in a deep pool, because I was just learning how to swim; also, I was convinced that I would get stuck in the tunneled portion of a waterslide, so the right one had to be completely uncovered to prevent certain death.

Eventually, I found it: the perfect slide. It met all the criteria, and the kids coming out of it seemed to be having the time of their lives. It was right next to one that seemed like it might be too much even for my half-wit brothers, launching people of all ages through the air to land in a seemingly bottomless pool. Plus it had a tunnel, so it was a miracle any of them survived.

As Mom escorted me by the hand up the long flight of stairs, I could feel the excitement building in my chest. When we reached the top, we found two separate lines. One was for the choice slide, and the other for the deviously constructed deathtrap. After making cer-

tain she was putting me in the right line, Mom told me she would be waiting for me at the bottom, and with a kiss for good luck, she headed back down the stairs.

Somehow a flock of butterflies had flown down into my stomach without me realizing it, and they were causing my heart to beat harder and faster than it ever had before. What was this intoxicating feeling, I thought to myself? No wonder Billy and Tommy are always trying to get themselves killed! This is incredible!

My inner monologue and excitement distracted me as, one by one, the people in front of me crossed their arms and legs and flew down the slide. Before I knew it, it was my turn. I was too nervous to look down, so I took a glance around and found a very curious sight. The line for the other slide was full of kids around my age and size, while my line was full of grown-ups. "That's odd," I could almost hear myself say.

"You're up, kid," the lifeguard told me. With a brow furrowed in confusion, I obediently crossed my arms and legs, and before I knew it, I was soaring down my very first waterslide. What an extraordinary feeling! The air rushed through my hair; the water splashed all around me. I couldn't stop myself from grinning as I thought about how good it would feel to tell my brothers about my heroism. That grin quickly disappeared, however, as I noticed a dark hole fast approaching me in my descent.

Soon darkness was all around me as I entered the tunnel that wasn't supposed to be there. My confusion quickly turned to horror as I felt the slide start to turn. Could it be that I had gotten on the wrong slide? Impossible—Mom put me on this one, and she would never do that. But she had.

The darkness left as quickly as it came, and I was able to catch my breath, thinking the worst of it was over. Then I remembered what lay at the bottom. I couldn't swim! I didn't have my trusted floaties! What was I going to do? Before I could find an answer, I was airborne, launched from the slide as it finished its run. My arms and legs flung defiantly as I tried to learn how to fly in order to save *myself. It didn't work. My last ditch effort to survive past the age of four failed. I looked down to see the deepest pool man had ever constructed, and if there were a shark waiting to greet me with its jaws wide open, I still could not have been more afraid.*

As I thrashed around in the water, struggling to keep my head up, I could hear Mom screaming. The remarkably capable lifeguard managed to stop admiring his tanned abs long enough to extend a pole out to me, which I clung onto for dear life as he pulled me out of the water.

I wouldn't say it was traumatizing per se, but then again I couldn't really say anything at all for a couple hours afterward. My heroic tale would have to be shared with Tommy and Billy another day. It would take a while for my baby steps to catch up with their leaps and bounds.

Vacations come and go, but the good times live on in the memories.

The Bottom Line

Wrap your kids in family. Give them a powerful sense of belonging to you and their siblings. Let them relish in the security and comfort of having you as a mom. Make your family work for your kids. This doesn't just happen—it takes living life together.

Start with your evenings—give them to your kids. Be there with your little ones, and be there with your teenagers. Do the same on weekends. Fill them with time together with you. Then create special memories by spending time away with them, to help your family grow even closer.

It is Rule #3: "Put your kids first." Don't hesitate and don't hold back—just give yourself to them. Change your life every which way to get your kids in the center of it. Then keep them there. You are a single mom. Do your job. Give your kids a childhood that will carry them through life. They can make it, they too can thrive, but not without you—all of you.

Chapter Four

Strip Parenting Down to the Basics

Like many youngsters, five-year-old Tommy preferred the barefoot-and-shirtless look—a pair of comfortable shorts, and he was set. Most of the time this worked for me. It made him happy and kept the laundry down. It was all good.

One summer afternoon, right after he had finished off a cherry Popsicle, Tommy picked up his favorite weapon—a wooden ax—and went in search of friends down the street. He rang the bell of one possibility, and when his friend's mother came to the door, he asked, "Can Brian play?" Brian's mom told me later that when she opened that door her stomach sank. There was Tommy, red stuff all over his face and stomach, weapon in hand, and asking if he could play with her son. "Oh, my gosh," she thought. "Who was his first victim?"

I didn't tell her that sometimes Tommy woke up looking that same way. She already had enough doubts about my parenting skills.

When I was in my midtwenties, a book called *Passages* was published; it supposedly addressed different stages of life. The book was very popular, so people would ask one another, "Where are you in your life?" I dismissed the whole idea as New Age nonsense. But when I became a single mom, I recalled the book and put a name on my "passage"—I called it "survival."

The term perfectly applied. I no longer cared if I excelled or did the extraordinary; I just wanted to be a good mom and see my kids succeed. But the future worried me—and I constantly thought about it. How would I ever be able to take care of these kids? What would happen if one of them were to get sick? Where would I find the money to keep paying the mortgage? Where would we be in five years? For that matter, where would we be in six months?

Looking forward and seeing nothing but the vast unknown unsettled me. Often after the divorce, I found myself scared for my boys— but I could do nothing but worry. So what was the point? No matter how I felt at night I still had to get up in the morning and take care of whatever faced me that day. That was reality—today. Not next week or next year—just today. This, I realized, I could do. And so I started to live my life the only way I could—one day at a time.

Each morning I would review what was ahead of me that day and would tell myself not to worry about anything else—it could wait. Survive today. That's it, nothing more. Then I'd set out to get it done. Some days went smoothly, but just as often they didn't. With three boys, anything could go wrong. I learned to expect the unexpected and act as if nothing that happened was out of the ordinary—to move with it, to get any situation under control and to call in resources if I couldn't do it alone. Just keep moving forward. The kids had to always know I could handle whatever happened.

As the months passed my confidence grew. I could do this—I could take care of my kids. Whatever the future held, it could only come at us one day at a time. Over the years when friends asked me, "How are you doing it?" I told them the truth: "One day at a time."

Surviving meant keeping my wits about me for fourteen-hour periods, until the kids went to bed. Then I could take a breather and regroup. My long-term planning—when I dared—took me right into the weekend. But even then I had to stay flexible. No telling what could happen between now and then.

At night I'd get the boys in bed and feel relief. We had made it through another day. The boys may have gone to bed dirty; they may have gone to bed late—maybe both. But that didn't matter—they were asleep. Don't get me wrong: getting the boys to bed on time was important to me, and I certainly wanted them clean before they hit the sheets. But these things didn't always happen, just as the daily "to do" list didn't always get done. Routine—as essential as it was—was the first casualty of a tough day. I had to adjust and make the tough calls. And then I had to let it go, not beat myself up or put more pressure on the kids. The important thing was that my kids were safely tucked in their beds. All was good for now—I would tackle tomorrow when the sun came up.

Sitting alone in my room, I would spend a few minutes thinking about the day—enjoying the good moments all over again and then considering what I could have done better. It was on-the-job-training, after all. I needed to learn from my mistakes if I was to improve tomorrow. But as for today—I did my best, and it was done.

If you're a single mom, or just a mom who feels like one—and life seems to be overwhelming, know that you too can make it, you too can survive—by taking it one day at a time.

But even then you are still only one parent doing the job of two. So you have to make certain you're spending your time and energy focused on the important stuff and not letting the insignificant tie you up. Here's how you do that.

Cut Your Expectations

Before I had children I would often look around at the kids at church and think how great my little ones would look one day—all decked out in their Sunday best. The girls would have pigtails with ribbons, and matching smocks. The boys would wear tough-guy hiking boots, khakis, and white oxford shirts. They would be well-behaved, polite, and smart-looking kids, and I would be so proud.

One Sunday, years later, I sat with my three boys at church and took inventory. These kids could have been little Irish orphans. Their clothes looked to have been retrieved from the bottom of a hamper, their socks hung loosely around their ankles, and the laces on the worn tennis shoes were barely tied. The older two pushed and shoved each other throughout the service, and when that didn't work, they threw a few punches. "Knock it off," I whispered, as I used my eyes to send a message of imminent bodily harm if they didn't obey.

Sunday school followed this service, and when I picked Billy up from his class, the teacher told me to check behind his ears. I would need a heavy cloth and strong soap, she added, to get him clean. Indignantly I took a peek—she had me nailed.

Here I was, the former Treasurer of the United States, and my boys were dirty little ruffians. Forget the well-mannered, well-groomed part—just plain "clean" appeared to be above my grade level.

Before kids it all seemed so simple. In my dreams I'd put their clothes out in the morning—clean, fresh, and matching, of course. Then I'd feed them a yummy, nourishing breakfast. The day would be spent in those organized activities that help children develop their talents and social skills. In the evening I'd have them brush their teeth and take baths. And then I'd read to them before bed or they'd read on their own. What was so hard about this?

I couldn't have been more clueless. Those ideals were too high for any parent. But even reasonable two-parent standards don't apply if you're raising kids alone. How could they—there's only one of you. You can't do it all, no matter how hard you try. So you have to pick the important stuff and let the rest go. Otherwise you're setting yourself up for failure.

It didn't take me long to realize that I had to cut my expectations significantly, both the ones for me and the ones for my kids. Clothes on their bodies, food in their stomachs, church on Sundays, and school on time—these were reasonable goals. Team sports used up energy, taught great lessons, and reduced idle time. I kept those. Scouts took too much of my time and took me away from the other two. We dropped it and never looked back.

To make this new life work I had to strip parenting down to the basics—no frills or shiny shoes. The boys needed to be fed, yes, but cereal worked fine (even for dinner, when necessary). As for clothes, I was humbled by the way my kids dressed. My priorities were good manners and good grades—the boys' rooms were a mess, but I learned not to care. They might be ragamuffins, but, what the heck, they never used bad language. I couldn't fight every battle, so I picked the important ones and let the kids run free of the others.

Take clean rooms, for instance. For the first couple years I put this right near the top of my "must have" list. But as the kids grew older, the resistance became formidable. What's more, they were never going to meet my standard for cleanliness.

It was a constant battle. They did a little and called it enough. I said more, and we were back at it. I couldn't keep it up—and it was dumb to keep trying. I had to stop, and so I did—with some caustic comment like, "If you want to live in squalor, be my guest." I didn't say I was a gracious loser, did I?

I called off the war, but I still cared. To keep my sanity I stayed clear of their rooms. It was the "what I don't see can't bother me" approach. For the most part we had a truce. Stuart was the worst—every square inch of his floor was covered—parts with several layers. When I needed to put clothes away, I made him give me a path to the dresser. He always obliged by moving his arm in a sweeping motion back and forth across the floor. I took Lamaze-like-breaths as I entered the room and kept my focus on the dresser. This lasted for years. One day I will have to apologize to his wife.

If truth be known, I became a better mom when I became a single parent. I no longer put unnecessary pressure on my kids or myself. I stopped caring what other families had or other people thought. My circumstances were different from theirs, and I had to make decisions according to what worked for us. I didn't need anyone else's approval—and I didn't seek it.

But when someone looked askance or made a comment, I turned into the Mama Bear.

In our Virginia home we had a self-designated Neighborhood Dad who was determined to get into my boys' business. He would catch them doing something he thought wrong, like throwing rocks through the windows of the partially built new homes in the neighborhood, and haul them home to me. Then he would ask what I was going to do to punish them. Well, that was information he was never going to get. It was a family matter, between my kids and me. I would assure him I'd get to the bottom of the problem, and then turn to the boys— and their friends—and tell them to go into the house. Once out of earshot of the nosy neighbor I'd get their side of the story and take whatever action I deemed appropriate. My first impulse was to have the boys egg the man's house. (And, by the way, the kids explained they were only throwing rocks at the already broken windows. It is possible, you know.)

This man believed my kids were juvenile delinquents, and that I was the permissive, clueless single mom. He underestimated us all, but I decided he could think what he wanted. The boys were my responsibility, and I wasn't sharing that job with the likes of him. My family was in order—I knew that—no matter how it looked from the outside.

No justification, no explanation, no rationalization—not to anyone. I only cared about the kids. Were they healthy and happy? Did they feel secure and confident? Were they respectful? Did they feel loved? And were they at least moving in the direction of well behaved? That is what mattered. And I could do that. I could make certain my kids had a solid foundation for a good life.

I had to pick what was important for my family, and you have to do the same for yours. No one else can do it for you. There are lots of good and commendable standards, but they're not all essential. Don't be afraid to toss some overboard—no matter if it's what your mom did or your best friend does or what your former self planned on doing. You can't do it all—and if you want to succeed as a single parent, you best not try.

The first step is to examine your expectations and then start chopping. Eliminate all thoughts of perfection—and while you're at it toss out "nearly perfect" as well. It doesn't exist in our world. You need a new game plan, an updated, streamlined version, one that works realistically for you and your kids. Keep only what matters most, and get rid of the rest. After a few months repeat this step, and keep cutting until you have found the right balance for your family.

For me it came down to a simple choice: time with my boys or racing around trying to keep up with the Joneses. Unrealistic standards were downright stupid when put into this context. Time with the kids was too short as it was; I needed to make what little I had work for us as best I could.

Good parenting is all about eliminating extraneous demands on your time and energy so you can give your kids what they need the most—security, a sense of belonging, a good family, and a life full of love and fun. Don't worry if your home isn't as tidy as your sister's or if your kids aren't enjoying homemade meals like your mom's. This is your family—you have to make tough decisions for your kids' sake. It's what parenting demands.

And remember: being smart doesn't have guilt as a side effect. So forget about carrying any of that poisonous stuff along with you for this ride.

Simplify Your Life

A good friend, who had three boys as well, told me she only bought white sports socks, the same brand every time. After doing the wash she threw all socks into the "sock box"—no pairing necessary. When the kids needed socks they would go to the box and pick out two. She knew they would match. I asked her what she did about dark socks for dress? She said white worked fine. Her boys went to college never having worn anything but white athletic socks. She had saved herself hundreds of hours of matching and folding socks. It was brilliant.

Unfortunately I heard this little nugget too late to implement in my own home. After years of going barefoot, Tommy developed a heightened sense of touch and became particular about the socks he wore. Because I was unable to figure any of this out myself, I had to take him to different stores, where he would put his hand inside dozens of socks and usually reject them. "They have to feel right," he would say, "or I can't wear them." I hope he has a kid just like him.

But I did pick up some valuable hours when I abandoned my mother's incredibly high standard for homemade dinners. She was an amazing cook and an even more impressive baker. When I think about my childhood, I remember coming down the stairs in the mornings to one of my favorite hot breakfasts. A cake or a couple pies would already be in the oven, and on the counter sat eight to ten lunch bags, packed with thick meaty sandwiches, potato chips, and homemade cookies, brownies, or a large piece of triple-decker chocolate cake. On Fridays lunch was tuna fish sandwiches along with all the goodies. One of my brothers would sometimes ask Mom for an extra dessert so he could trade up or sell it. (He became a lawyer.)

I made it easy for Mom—no sandwich Monday through Thursday, just peanut butter crackers. Tuna worked fine for Fridays. Even though our names were on the brown paper bags, I would still occasionally get the wrong one. Don't know how, as the boys' lunches weighed in at about five pounds. But when it happened, I would open the bag at lunchtime and gag. I couldn't even look at the monstrous sandwich. But I wasn't worried. I knew somewhere in the school one of my brothers was staring at peanut butter crackers—he'd be around shortly.

Mom fed eleven mouths once again at dinner, and every night we ate a balanced meal: meat, potatoes or rice, vegetables, bread, and a homemade dessert. We never had pizza. There was no way I could match her. As fine a tradition as it was, and as great as it would have been for my boys, I couldn't manage it most of the time—not even with only a third the kids.

Instead I did take a few of her recipes and treated my kids to them regularly. I learned to make her spaghetti sauce, for instance, and would make a double batch—we would eat it for lunch or dinner for days. And like Mom, I loved to bake, so homemade cookies were a common sight in our home. But so were mac 'n' cheese, Spaghetti-Os, and pizza. I would make the boys drink a glass of milk with these meals to calm my conscience.

Once, a friend told me Wednesday was pancake night in her home. *What a terrific idea,* I thought—*simple and easy.* I tried it. My kids balked, "This is breakfast food, Mom. Where is dinner?" So I got out the Hot Pockets—they were easier than pancakes anyhow.

Did I feel good about this radical drop in standards from my parent's home? No. But I was a single mom, and I had to find the time to be a good one. So I simplified my life every way I could. It's why I let the boys dress themselves—one less thing on my list. Admittedly this came with a painful adjustment. I liked a clean, sharp look, and they couldn't have cared less; comfort was all that mattered to them. Every couple days I'd make certain the clothes on the floor (the boys never used hampers—another guy thing, I think) were washed. Then for school, church, and special occasions I required a higher standard—collared shirts and long pants. Pressed and spotless? Not so much.

Much to my amazement, my boys all eventually became remarkably good dressers. So the only damage was to my pride. At times I was downright embarrassed at how they looked. But I learned not to care. Instead I would laugh—at their clothes and at myself. It really was amusing if you looked at it in the right light.

Prioritize So You Can Pick Your Battles

My dad never tolerated foul language in our home. He didn't use it, and he wasn't about to hear it from his kids. I shared Dad's belief that there was no place for vulgarity in one's life; it served no positive purpose. I was determined to carry on this tradition in my own family, and so I made it one of my priorities. That meant it was worth the fight—there would be no backing down or compromising. In our home there would be no bad language.

The rule was simple: no taking the Lord's name in vain, no curse words, no trashy words, and no words that mean the same as any of the above. I even banned the word "crap." It was trash talk and therefore unnecessary.

I told the kids if they dared to use any of the forbidden words or expressions, I would wash their mouth out with soap. Not particularly original, I admit, but for a while it worked. That is until Tommy was six. Being a frequent offender, he grew accustomed to the taste of Dove. He would casually use an offensive word, take himself to the bathroom, take a bite of soap, yell to me that he had done the punishment, and go on his way.

Determined not to lose this battle, I increased the consequences. Soap was out; tomato juice was in. I loved the stuff, but every time I drank it all three boys would gag. The next time Tommy used a bad word I took him into the kitchen, poured a small glass of V-8 juice, and, with both brothers looking on in horror, made him drink the thick, red stuff. He took a sip but couldn't swallow—his body began to dry heave, making it impossible. I wasn't deterred—he wasn't leaving that kitchen until he managed to get a tablespoon of tomato juice down the hatch.

My kids knew I meant business when it came to vulgarity. The standard was high, but it was what I expected of them. There would be no negotiating on this issue, as Tommy came to learn when he was in fourth grade. He played on a basketball team and found that most kids used foul language. In hopes of fitting in better he asked if he could just have one bad word. "How about 'crap'?" he asked. I thought a moment and said, "No, no bad words—not even one."

Do I think for a moment that none of my boys ever used bad language? I know differently. But by making it a priority in our home, I taught them how important it was to me that they didn't. I showed them by both my words and actions that this principle was of great value—worthy of all my efforts to enforce while they were in my care. Later they would have to decide for themselves. But by then my job would be done. They would always know where I stood on the matter.

Today my kids don't use foul language, and it is not used in their homes. They also don't drink tomato juice.

I picked my battles. "Well dressed" and "clean rooms" didn't make the cut. "Good manners" and "clean mouths" did. How they looked in church wasn't an issue—that they were in church was. These were my decisions.

It's the same for every single mom or dad. You have to prioritize for your family. All standards aren't equal. You have to choose which ideals you believe are the most critical and then teach them to your children every day—through your words, your example, and your actions. These are the battles worth fighting—you can't lose them or you will lose your kids. Draw a line in the sand and let your children know that when it comes down to these principles—the ones you have decided are vitally important to your family—they will live them. Then make certain they do.

Keep the Small Problems Small

Baskin Robbins was a favorite spot of ours. One particularly hot summer afternoon, when Tommy was four years old, I decided it was just the treat we needed. An associate of mine, who was temporarily living at my home, joined us. She was single and had no children.

Our idea was anything but original—half the town was there. The little store was jammed, and the line flowed out onto the sidewalk. When our turn finally came, Tommy ordered and went outside with my friend, and they waited for the rest of us. Within minutes Tommy was back—I could hear him screaming his way through the crowd to tell me his ice cream had fallen out of the cone. The ice cream attendant had obviously not pushed the ice cream far enough into it to prevent the problem, but when she saw the distraught kid, she gave him another.

We joined the others outside, and all of us began to walk quietly along the sidewalk, fully engrossed in our chosen flavors. That's when I saw Tommy's new chocolate scoop come tumbling over the edge of his cone and fall smack onto the blistering concrete. Before Tommy could register this latest disaster I gave my cone to my associate, grabbed his empty one, and, in one fluid motion, scooped the ice cream off the ground in my hand and put it right back into his cone. I pressed it down to make certain there was no act three to this play, picked off all noticeable debris, and handed it back to him. Without a word he began to lick the ice cream and walk along his way. All was good in his world.

I didn't have so much as a twinge that anything out of the ordinary had happened until I saw the face of my friend—pure horror. Of course, she was shocked, I thought, *think what you just did.* Not long ago I would have been equally outraged, I reminded myself. But that was before I joined the ranks of motherhood. I couldn't let such a little problem get out of hand—not if I could stop it. "We do what we have to do to make it all work," I told her.

I wasn't always this way. When my oldest was born, I would find reasons to worry—wondering what was normal and what wasn't. I would call Mom and tell her my latest concern and ask her opinion. *She would know,* I thought, after all, she had nine children. After a few weeks of this nonsense she told me, "Bay, what you need is another kid." She had a point. By the time I was a single mom of three I never looked for problems. I didn't need to; they came looking for me.

The key to handling problems is to be able to distinguish the level of concern required. All of them are not equal, and the last thing any parent, especially a single one, needs to do is blow them out of proportion. You can't afford to add to your burden unnecessarily.

There are basically three kinds of problems—the big, tough, nasty ones that require close attention; the ones that can be nipped in the bud and eliminated; and the ones that should be ignored. Sometimes it's best to ride a new one for a while to see where it takes you. With time you get a better handle on its level of seriousness, and simple solutions often present themselves.

What you don't want to do is overreact or overdramatize. Solving problems is part of your job—don't make a big deal about it; just do it. Your kids take their cue from you. If you are calm, they will be. If you panic, you will make their situation worse, adding to their fear and anxiety. Take control. Deliberately and carefully assess the situation and then resolve it as quickly and quietly as possible.

I saw the effectiveness of this calm but direct approach to problems when my oldest boy went to third grade. Two issues that had the potential to be serious fell into my lap right on top of one another. It was a new school for Billy, and although this kind of transition can be tough for most kids, this child suffered from anxiety and that made it all the worse. First, Billy wasn't able to use the bathroom at the school. Second, he developed the nasty habit of chewing his T-shirt—the entire front side of it.

With respect to the bathroom, the poor kid would tell me that "You can see through the cracks in the stalls and I can't go." So he would drink nothing all day and then would run all the way home after school. It didn't take a genius to know this needed immediate attention. I talked to his doctor about this strange phenomenon only to learn that it wasn't that unusual for boys—some men even had the problem. (That was more information than I needed.) He advised me not to make much of it with my son. "Most likely he will grow out of it—and if he doesn't we'll deal with it then." It was such great advice.

In the meantime he recommended I check out the school. "Look for a private bathroom, the kind with a full door," he told me. "Where the nurse is you'll find one. Talk to her and see if she'll help you. It might not work," he warned, "but it's the simplest solution, so try it first."

The next day I went in search of the perfect bathroom. And just like the doc said, I found it in the nurse's station, which happened to be next to the desk of a school assistant. I started with her—one mom to another. Quietly I explained my son's predicament, pointed to the private bathroom a few feet away, and asked if she could help me out. It was the teacher's bathroom, she said, and against school policy for kids to use. Then she added, "But have him come see me. I'll take care of it." And that's just what the fine lady did. This problem was solved. (P.S. My son must have grown out of it—or maybe he just never talked to me about it again. Either way worked for me.)

But even with this issue resolved, Billy continued to eat his shirt. He would come home from school with the entire front of it wrinkled and wet. I would sometimes watch as he took the collar into his mouth and moved downward, chewing relentlessly as he went. I spoke with him casually about it and gave him a few weeks to stop. But though his progress at school was terrific and he loved his teacher and his class, the T-shirts kept coming home wet. It was an ugly habit, and I was determined to break it.

One night I took his favorite tees, soaked them in vinegar, and tossed them in the dryer. I called his teacher to tell her not to worry if my son smelled of vinegar for a few days, explaining what I had done. I solicited no advice—it was a simple heads up. I was going to nip this shirt-eating habit right in the bud, and that's just what I did—in two days flat.

At the core of both these problems was the new school. My son just needed my help until he could work things out for himself. But if handled differently, these issues could have led to meetings with his teachers and counselors. Billy didn't need any more attention to his problems than was absolutely necessary. I did due diligence by calling his doctor and then went about the business of putting both these issues behind us as quickly as possible—for both his sake and mine.

Life as a single mom is brutally challenging. Just getting the basics done is incredibly difficult, so you can't let the problems overwhelm you. You will have plenty of them—that's a given. So you have to take control of them, not let them take control of you. If an issue doesn't need your attention now, then watch it awhile. If it can be resolved quickly, then do it. But the one thing you should never do is let the little problems join the ranks of the big ones—not if you can prevent it.

The Bottom Line

Families are defined by the principles that are taught inside the home. Parents need to make a conscious decision what the defining values are going to be for their families—and then see to it that their kids are immersed in them. This is particularly difficult for single parents. You're only one person, but you have the job of two. But you can do it all—if you give yourself a chance. Cut your expectations, simplify your life, prioritize your battles, take control of problems, and live life as it comes—one day at a time.

It's all part of Rule #4: "Strip parenting down to the basics." It is the only way to be certain you are focusing your time and energy on the important stuff—and that's what being a single mom is all about.

Chapter Five

Give Your Kids a Home to Love

Like most kids, my boys believed in the Tooth Fairy. When one of their pearly whites came out, they'd put it under their pillow and during the night she'd come and replace it with a dollar. What's not to believe?

But the Tooth Fairy lost her esteemed position in our home one summer afternoon in Baltimore. We were on a family excursion at the city's famed aquarium. As always, Tommy was running through the crowds at top speed and took a spill. He smacked his mouth on a railing, split it open, and was screaming uncontrollably when I caught up with him. I cleaned him up in the ladies room and stopped the bleeding. But he was inconsolable.

I couldn't figure it out. This was a tough kid who rarely carried on like this. He was so upset, he couldn't even talk. I checked for broken bones and tried to calm him. "What's wrong, Sweetie?" I kept asking him. Finally he cried out, "I lost my tooth!" Still clueless, I told him it was okay. "No, it's not," he screamed. "How can the Tooth Fairy come if I don't have my tooth?" The light went on. I needed to find the baby tooth—or something that resembled it.

We returned to the scene of the accident—a darkly lit area in front of the sharks. After crawling around the legs of ill-humored tourists for several minutes, I knew this plan was going nowhere. I needed another.

I pulled out my wallet, took out a five-dollar bill, and handed it to the kid. "This is for your tooth," I said. "It's better than the Tooth Fairy." A huge smile came across Tommy's face, and he ran to tell his brothers that Mom had given him five dollars for his tooth. The going price for teeth went up that afternoon, and the Tooth Fairy was history. The kids had no need for her when they had me.

Fast forward eighteen months. Billy is around ten years old and has fallen in love for the first time. The lucky lady is a blond beauty in his Sunday School class. With Christmas fast approaching, he decides to get her a gift. When she learns of his intent, she lets slip that her birthday is a few days after Christmas. My instincts—those totally trustworthy ones that come from being a woman—screamed, "That's one big whopper!" But there was no telling Billy. Two special occasions required two gifts, he explained, not one. In an attempt to persuade him otherwise I offered to help with one good gift—but he was on his own for two.

He asked me how much money he would need for two gifts, and I told him about forty dollars if he wanted them both to be nice. But that doesn't matter, I insisted, because you only need to get one. Because he had no money, I was convinced I'd win this one.

Sometime later Billy found me in the kitchen. He handed me five baby teeth and said, "These are good for twenty-five dollars, Mom." I was horrified—but held my position. Good for one really fine gift, I told him, or two cheap ones. He left the room.

An hour later he returned with two more teeth! Concerned the permanent kind were his next target I agreed he could get two gifts and took him to the mall. (I also suggested he keep his mouth shut when he gave the little vixen her presents—wouldn't want to scare her off!)

———

There are so many amazing stories that took place inside the four walls my boys and I called home. But then again, that is how it should be.

After all, it was where my boys started life and lived it, where they met their brothers and learned to love, where they grew strong and tall and close. In short, it was where we became a family.

The environment inside their home means everything to children. It is as important to them as the air they breathe and the food they eat. It should be like a giant security blanket wrapped tightly around them, providing them at every stage of development with a powerful sense of belonging and a guaranteed refuge from the outside world.

For kids to thrive, their home has to be a place where they feel the comfort and confidence that comes with being part of something bigger and better than themselves. Surrounded by loved ones they grow up knowing they are not alone in this world that there will always be someone close by to teach them what they need to know, help them through the tough days, and pick them up when they fall. They learn their home isn't just where they live—it is where they belong because it is where their family lives.

I remember as a young girl walking into my home after school, knowing that dinner would be at 6 p.m. sharp, that I would sit in my place on Mom's immediate right, and that all eleven of us would remain standing until Dad said Grace. I knew how it all worked inside this house, what the rules were, and what was expected of me. I knew this is where the people lived who most cared for me. It was ground zero for all that was good in my life, and I was determined to create the same for my kids.

Every child deserves a good home. But they don't just happen—it's up to you to create it. First you need to choose the kind of world you want your children to grow up in, and then you need to build it. Will it be warm and friendly, happy and comfortable, loving and nurturing? Or will it be demanding, stressful, and contentious? It's your call.

What goes on inside the walls of the home defines a family—for better or for worse. Kids need familiarity, interaction, and closeness with you and their siblings. They thrive on lots of love and plenty of discipline. It's like putting together a football team. And as a single mom you're both coach and quarterback, the kids are your teammates, and your home is the field—it's where your team learns to work together and become a family. You need to be there with them, encouraging and instructing and making it fun. No one else can do it—only you.

And remember: a good home is essential to the healthy emotional development of your kids. So put them first and design your home around their interests, not yours.

Below I give you some insight into how I did this for my kids. But remember, what works for one family doesn't necessarily work for another. Each home takes on the character of the family inside—no two are alike.

But there are some steps that you must take and a few rules that you have to enforce if you want to give your kids the kind of home they need and deserve. The first one is to establish a family space in your home and then drive the kids there, all of them—even the teenagers.

Create a Family-Centered Home

Tommy played baseball in seventh and eighth grade, and I attended most of his games. I would try to sit next to the parents of one of the star players so I could chat. I liked them both, and because what was happening on the field bored me silly, I was anxious to find a pleasant distraction.

After a while the mom came only when the dad couldn't. On those days she and I would talk our way through one inning after another, stopping only when one of our boys was at bat. Halfway through one of the seasons she told me she was leaving her husband and her home. Her two sons would continue to live with their dad, but she would remain actively involved in their lives. "I have no family life," she explained. "We don't even eat dinner together. I make a meal, put it on the plates, and they pick it up and take it to their bedrooms."

I couldn't understand what she was saying. My kids weren't allowed to take snacks or drinks to their bedrooms, much less a meal.

In fact, they didn't even leave the dinner table until they asked to be excused and I consented.

Something was clearly amiss, but I couldn't put my mind around it.

I asked her to explain what she meant, and she described life in her home. Each of her sons had a television, a computer, and the latest game system set up in their bedrooms. Not surprisingly, when her kids were home, whether for dinner or whatever else, that's where they went. If their friends came over, they all hung out in the bedrooms. (Her husband had a similar habit. When he came home, he took his dinner to the room that housed his toys.) *Amazing,* I thought. She turned her kids' bedrooms into individual entertainment centers and was alarmed when that's where they chose to live!

These friends had a big, beautiful house, richly decorated inside and out—yet it wasn't a home. They had plenty of money and were generous with their kids—but you can't buy a family. You have to invest gobs of together-time to get one of those. These boys, like all kids, needed a childhood filled with family time. Instead they were given expensive toys, which they used to entertain themselves—alone in their separate rooms.

To be a family you have to live like one. Group activities have to be the norm, not the exception. This precious structure needs constant care and attention to be strong and vibrant. It doesn't just spring to life when a baby is born. It is built with hard work and sacrifice from the ground up, one block at a time.

I don't know what my friend was thinking. Was she giving the kids what she thought would make them happy—the best of everything, all set up and organized in their private rooms? Or was she trying to preserve the clean, orderly, and tasteful nature of her house by giving her boys their own space? Maybe it's how her husband wanted it. I don't know and it doesn't matter. What does matter is that her kids never got the home they needed.

Especially as a single parent, you can't make this mistake. Your kids desperately need the grounding that comes with strong family ties. That means you need to establish a home that is family centered, one that is specifically designed to drive all of you together. Then add a few rules that give your kids no other option than to be together. Only you can do this.

Though not hard, it can be tough. But that's no excuse for failing. You just have to learn to say "no" to your kids, mean it, and don't back down. Your kids need a home that is all about family—their family. And it's your responsibility to give them one.

Let's talk about how that's done.

Bedroom

In spite of what the general trend might suggest, kids don't need their own bedrooms. There is nothing wrong and plenty right about sharing one with a sibling or two. Bedtime play and lights-out conversations are special times for kids and can lead to stronger ties between brothers or sisters. And the memories created are invaluable.

In *Right from the Beginning,* my brother Pat writes about his experience in a crowded bedroom. "For a child to have a room of his own may be ideal, but I would not trade those eight years in that same room with my three brothers for the Lincoln Bedroom. They cemented bonds of affection that have lasted all our lives."

Although it may not work for your family, kids who share bedrooms are often the lucky ones.

But whether the bedrooms in your home have one, two, or four kids in them, none should have televisions, computers, iPads, or game systems. It takes children away from the family when what you most want—and they most need—is to be drawn into it. Bedrooms should be reserved for limited activity—so design them that way. Give your children little reason to want to spend large amounts of time in the privacy of their own room.

Instead put these electronic devices in a common area—where everyone can be involved. That will bring the kids out of their rooms and put them smack in the middle of the family. It doesn't matter if they like it or not—it's up to you. You decide what's best for them and then make it happen. There is simply no dispute that kids should never be isolated for long periods of time. They need constant contact with their siblings—and with you when you're home—if you are going to be a family. And this will happen when you close the door to all other options.

If you scratch the surface of the arguments made for electronic toys in a child's bedroom—spun as making life wonderful for the little ones—you will see that it isn't about the kids; it's about the parents. These devices are magnets used to take children out of the living space of the adults. Who of us wouldn't prefer to move the mess that seems to travel right behind our kids out of sight to their private rooms? Who of us wouldn't prefer to have those obnoxious war games played out of earshot? And who of us wouldn't prefer not to have to share our television with the kids every night of the week? It's oh-so tempting. But that doesn't mean you do it—not if you are about building a family.

Face it: kids are loud and obnoxious; they create havoc and messes. But the noise and chaos are worth it because, while they're making it, they're building bonds that will last a lifetime. You don't do that playing Nintendo alone in your bedroom.

It's a sacrifice to have a family-centered home—one you make for your kids. You put your interests second to theirs, and you do everything in your power to give them a close and loving environment in which to live every day of their lives. Give your kids a good home, one that constantly brings them all together. Everyone eats together, watches TV together, plays games together—there's no escaping it. It's how things are done in your home.

Computers

In spite of what they tell you, kids don't need their own laptops. A family computer—or two—will work fine. You may choose to get them their own and, as a result, homework hours in your home might run smoother. But I couldn't afford more than one when my kids were young. And there is a definite advantage to having more than one person using a single computer: it provides human monitoring. My boys loved to snoop around into the others' business, and I quickly learned the benefits.

Within weeks of getting a computer, Tommy, who was twelve, was excited about a neat girl from New Jersey who was "chatting" with him. His older brother suggested he do some research on her and showed him how. The thirteen-year-old girl turned out to be a thirty-five-year-old man! Needless to say, new restrictions were immediately imposed on computer conversations. This was years before Facebook, but even today supervision is critical when it comes to kids and computers.

Whatever you decide about the number of computers in your home, do not allow your kids to use them in the privacy of their own rooms—not under any circumstance. It is never necessary and always foolhardy. Not only does it undermine your efforts to create a family-centered home, but it can also be dangerous. Do not risk it. Set down the law as early as you can—preferably when your little babes are still in their cribs—and never back down. Here it is: all computers in your home are to be used only in the area you designate. The one require-ment for you is to choose a highly traveled family space. It could be the kitchen, a family room, or even a hallway. The kids either follow the rule or don't use the computers. Give them no other choice. And by the way, it's a family rule—which means it also applies to you. The greatest lessons in life are taught by example.

The kitchen is often a good place for the family computer to live. Plenty of traffic there, which will encourage your kids to view only ap-propriate websites. Also, this situation invites conversation. While you are cooking or folding clothes, you can ask: How was school today? Would you look up a recipe for me? Did you hear about a particular event in the news? They may want to look up the story and get the details. Or the two of you might laugh about a Facebook entry or a YouTube video. You are casually together with your child—the pos-sibilities are endless.

Some of my readers may stop at this point and think: that horse is out of the barn and running wild in the pasture—my kids already have computers in their bedroom. Well, take them out of there. I know, I know—this could incite a revolt, bring about a complete breakdown of communications, and set off a total meltdown of your sweet teenager. Kids are good at getting what they want; I don't deny it. They may even dive into their handy toolbox and pull out those insidious questions: "Why are you doing this? Don't you trust me?" (My boys learned young never to go there.)

This line of argument is so overrated. Fall for it once and they'll beat you over the head with it right up to the moment you catch the little con artists breaking your rules.

Simply tell them, "That's irrelevant." Your job as a parent isn't to make your kids feel you trust them, for goodness sake. It is to love them so much that you do what is right for them, no matter how difficult. Enforcing rules is part of that. Good parenting requires that you decide what's best for your kids, establish the rules that will make this happen in your home, and then see to it that your kids obey them.

Depending on their age, some kids view a computer in their room as a privacy right or some such nonsense. They may also feel awkward being on the computer with siblings or you nearby. That's when you know you're onto something. Whatever you do, don't let them win this one—it is worth the fight and it's critical to your kids that you prevail. Enforce the rule. All computers in your home must be kept in the designated family space at all times. If they persist, just tell them, "You don't like it, don't use the computer."

This is one of the important battles. The good news is: you will win. The kids will moan and groan, but they will follow the computers. Then you will have them where they should be—even if for the first couple weeks it's the last place you want them. Enforcing this rule will keep you closer to your children and better informed about what they're up to.

Family Space

Family areas should be stress-free and relaxing for all of you. It's where you want your kids to hang out and spend most of their time. So plan accordingly—with dirty shoes, sweaty bodies, and Nerf-gun battles in mind. For these rooms expensive and fashionable is out; comfortable and cleanable is in. Kids don't appreciate lovely—they don't care that

the rug is an oriental; they're still going to knock their drinks onto it.
And as for the family heirloom on the mantel, it won't even cause them
to pause before tossing the football.

Design family space around your kids being kids. Then, when they
are, you will laugh and not cry. By the time Tommy was three I knew I
had a spiller on my hands. It was guaranteed. Every first milkshake I
ever gave the kid lived out its life in the rug. So I covered the floors in
my family room with cheap carpet remnants so it wouldn't bother me.
After a hundred or so accidents I'd just buy a new remnant and we'd
start over. Spills were part of life in our home, so I accommodated them.

The center of our home was the den. The room was all about comfort—big, cozy couches and chairs with throws everywhere. You could
easily sleep there, and friends often did—for weeks at a time. There
was a ton of board games, a bookcase full of old movies, and, in the
corner, a big screen TV. It was made for family time. Smoothies, popcorn, John Wayne, the kids, and me all together in the den—life didn't
get better than that for this single mom.

Here's how Stuart describes our family space:

*When I think of my house, I see multicolored brick outside, outlined
by the woods around it; I see the cracked driveway and the messy
garage; I see trees and animals and chores that need to be done. But
when I think of home, I think of the one room around which all the
others revolved, the hub, or as the ridiculous sign Mom hung in it
once I'd left for college reads, "The Gathering Place." It was our
room, and Mom wanted it that way. She understood that us kids felt
out of our element in a perfectly clean room, so she always permitted
a small measure of disorder. My friends called the couches "Vampire
Couches" because once you laid down, they sapped your energy and
you never wanted to get back up. The fireplace, dark bookcases, and
wooden beams overhead created the ideal room in which to pass the
time. Of course, the big-screen TV didn't hurt either. Just as the stupid sign said, it was a "Gathering Room"—the den for a Mama
Bear's cubs; but above all, it was home.*

I did put that sign in the room after he left. But it wasn't stupid. It meant the world to me because it reminded me of all those good times with my boys—gathered together in our favorite room.

The kids used to just gravitate there—whether it was after school or before bed, that's where you'd find them. And because there were three of them and only one TV, the situation required that they deal with one another. I set down one rule—whoever was in the den first chose the channel for the first hour, then it rotated to the next kid in the room. If this didn't work for the majority, negotiations would commence, usually followed by intimidation and coercion. What can I say: I was preparing them for a life in politics—just in case.

I must admit that at some point I turned the basement into a game room, and to be honest, this was as much about what was good for the boys as it was good for me. My justification was simple: it wasn't in the boys' interest for me to lose my mind.

A half-dozen screaming boys, playing hours of video games while dozens of wires hung on the TV set—I couldn't do it. I had to move the scene out of my line of vision. So I gave the boys' a game room in the basement—Ping Pong, pool, and a good-sized TV for their video games. On weekends and during summers it would fill up with kids— some at the pool table, others playing video games—all taking their turns, being loud and rowdy, and loving life. But they always closed the day in the den lounging and snacking while they talked and laughed about everything and anything. Then it was movie time.

As a mom you want, above all, for your kids to have a good home. So give them a place where they love to be. Design it around them— comfortable, fun, and family oriented. And then join them there.

Create a Magical World for Your Kids

I had this theory about boys based on nothing but instinct and personal observation. Here's how it went. As boys become teenagers they withdraw emotionally and many become self-conscious and uncomfortable about hugging and kissing loved ones. Whether this phenomenon worked itself out over the years mattered little to me. I was not taking any chances; I was going to keep my boys hugging right into their twenties.

My plan involved the wonderful world of four-legged creatures. I knew once these furry little guys got ahold of their hearts, my boys would never turn a cold shoulder to them, no matter what their age. And I was right.

Unfortunately my plan ran amok somewhere along the way, and I lost total control. It's not to say it didn't work, because it did. But although the number of kids remained the same, the number of pets just kept climbing until we maxed out at about seven. As I said, I lost control.

It all started the first Christmas we were without a dad. I bought Siamese kittens for my two oldest boys, who were three and four years old at the time. Billy named them Kraken and Kong, and there was no turning back. Our home became pet haven for the next twenty years. Every kid had at least one dog and a couple of cats to call their own. And if one died, the boys begged for another. What could I do?

First it was cats. We started with the two, but sadly the coyotes nabbed one and a garage door the other. So we bought another, a female kitten we named Kasha. She was a particularly friendly animal—especially with the local tomcats. Within weeks she was pregnant. The boys were mesmerized watching the birth of each of her four kittens. The problem was that they became attached—and so did I. So we kept Kasha's family together and turned our home into a magical place for the boys.

But it didn't stop there.

Before I could get Kasha to an operating table she slipped out to say "hi" to her friends, leaving her kittens to fend for themselves for a few hours. That's all it took and we had another seven kittens on the way. After this litter was born I put Kasha under house arrest until the big day at the vet's office—it was circled in red on the calendar.

About the same time our nanny, who was living with us off and on, was given a puppy as a gift. That put the number of pets in our home at thirteen for the summer. Much to the pure delight of my youngsters, I had turned our home into a petting zoo. Every morning the neighborhood kids would line up to see the animals; one mother caustically suggested I charge a fee.

Concerned my neighbors would begin to refer to me as "the cat lady," I dumped the seven new kittens off at the vet's as soon as they were old enough to leave their momma. Five cats were plenty, even by my standards. Someone else could enjoy the others.

Then came the dogs. To sweeten the move to Virginia I told Tommy I would get him a dog. As an eight-year-old boy, he couldn't have been more excited. That's when we added Spike, an Australian sheepdog, to our family. A few years later Stuart adopted an English sheltie named Nicky. Not long after that a French poodle named Scamp joined the ranks.

But though I admit that the idea of all these animals was nothing short of crazy, they really did bring out the best in my boys. Each pet had their own distinct personality, and they became members of our family. The kids would hug and squeeze them by day and snuggle and sleep with them by night.

It didn't matter to Billy that he woke up sneezing every morning; he loved to have his cat sleep right on his head. And although my oldest preferred the felines to the dogs, Tommy and Stuart loved them all. Tommy would often go to bed with both Spike and Nicky under the blankets with him. Stuart would come home from school and go immediately to the floor of the kitchen, where he'd wrestle with the dogs until they grew tired. Then he'd settle in for a little TV or Nintendo with his cat Lilly, nicknamed "The Loon" for good reason, on his shoulders.

A few years ago Nicky contracted cancer and needed to be put to sleep. This dog had come to live with us when my youngest son was just turning eight years old. Stuart was terrified of Tommy's big powerful animal and was having some difficulty with life in general. I felt he needed something he could love unconditionally—something that was all his. So for his birthday we went in search of a dog.

When we found Nicky, he was emaciated, could not bark, and had been abused. Because he was in such bad shape, the vet thought he might be in the advanced stages of cancer. But Stuart loved that dog back to health, and Nicky paid him back with years of comfort and companionship. When I told Stuart that Nicky was going to have to be put down, he said it was okay. "He did his job, Mom. He got me through some of the toughest years of my life." How do you put a price on this?

Whenever the boys came through the front door, they were greeted by a cadre of excited animals. Who wouldn't be happy with such a welcome? These pets provided endless entertainment and kept my three tough boys hugging and loving right through their teen years. They became part of our family, and they added enormously to the character of our home—if not the charm.

Although pets are certainly not for everyone, those six dogs and ten cats who lived out their lives with us helped make our two homes magical places for my boys. As crazy as it sounds, filling our home with furry animals worked for my family. Your job is to find what works for yours, because giving your kids a home that is magical will bring joy and happiness right through your front door.

Make Their Friends Feel at Home

As a youngster I was painfully shy and often felt ill at ease in the homes of friends. I can still remember standing in the kitchen of one of my little pals and trying to find the courage to ask for a glass of water. My friend would get herself a drink or her mom would get one for her. Seldom did anyone ask if I would like one. This happened dozens of times, and each time I got this sick feeling that tore away at my fragile self-confidence. I could never understand why her mom always made me ask. Why didn't she just offer or at least make some gesture that would make me feel welcomed in their home? But she never did, and I never forgot how awful it felt.

Kids don't deserve that. They have enough issues to deal with in their young lives. After my own experience I was determined that no child would ever feel that way in my home.

Decades later, when I lived in California, my neighbor Pam told me that whenever I drove down the street to my home, "it's like the pied piper has arrived. All these little kids see your car and come running behind you." It was just the way I wanted it.

When the boys were young, I taught them that their friends were always welcomed in our home—they didn't need to ask permission to invite them. It was their home, and they could have their buddies over anytime they liked. Basically we had an open-door policy.

Then I gave their pals plenty of reasons to come. There were milkshakes and homemade cookies at snack time, plenty to eat at lunch or dinner, and their own refillable bowl of popcorn at night. I asked their friends to join us for trips to the park, the pool, or the movies. If we went on a bike trip, I waited for them to get their bikes, brought water bottles for them, and treated them to McDonalds.

My boys also understood that, in our home, friends were treated like family. Everyone played together—brothers and friends alike—and no one was ever made to feel uncomfortable. It was a rule that I seldom needed to enforce because it was how my kids learned to live since the time they could walk.

The first week of kindergarten four-year-old Tommy met his first best friend, Angel. Immediately they became inseparable. Angel had a beautiful older sister, Linda, who happened to be Billy's age, and they lived around the corner from us. They were also being raised by a single mom and these two siblings never stopped looking out for one another. For the next four years, until we moved to Virginia, Angel and Linda lived at our home most weekends and throughout the summers—all day and all night. They did everything with us; they were family, and our home was a better place because of it.

When the boys were older, I would tell their friends to help themselves to anything they found in the kitchen—there was no need to ask. Then I'd stock the place. If I was home, I'd fix them meals; if I wasn't, they were to do it themselves.

My kids loved having their friends in their home, and I felt the same way—it meant I knew where my kids were and I knew their friends. It was a perfect arrangement, so I gave my kids a home that their friends loved as much as they did.

Here are Stuart's thoughts on the matter:

My house was my home. That may sound redundant, but it's the truth. My house wasn't just a building where I ate, slept, and lived. It was where I always wanted to eat, sleep, and live. And I wasn't the only one; my friends felt the same way, and if any of them try to deny it, ask them how many days they spent at their own homes during the summer. This wasn't due to any fault of their parents by any means; indeed, my friends' families were every bit as wonderful as my own. And my house was hardly the biggest, or the cleanest, or the nicest. But we loved it, and that made all the difference, even if at times it made no sense at all.

One such occasion happened during the summer after my friends and I graduated from high school. During those three months, for all intents and purposes, my best friends, Joe and Nico, lived at my house. YouTube was just taking off around this time, and suddenly we had unlimited access to all of our favorite shows, in fifteen-minute segments. After several hours huddled around a laptop screen, Joe came up with the brilliant idea of hooking the computer up to the big-screen TV.

After a quick trip to Best Buy, we were living the dream. Tall, ice-cold glasses of Cran-Apple: check. Endless hours of entertainment: check. The world's most comfortable couches: check. Air-conditioned protection from the brutally humid Virginia summer: che-oh, wait, forget that last one. You see, for as long as I can re-

member, for one week of every summer our air conditioning decided to take a vacation of its own. "It's okay," Mom would say. "Just put a fan in the window and it'll blow all the cold air in." I don't know where she gets her ideas, but when the air outside might as well be on fire, blowing it inside is what most people call a "bad idea."

Now, most people, when faced with volcanic climate conditions within their own home, would decide to maybe drive fifteen minutes down the road to one of the many other available options for watching illegally uploaded television shows. Joe, Nico, and I are not "most people." We gathered all the fans in the house, opened all the windows, and shut the doors leading to the den. I took one couch, Nico the other, and Joe laid on the floor, each armed with our own fan and significantly less-than-ice-cold glasses of Cran-Apple. As the hours wore on and the summer inferno continued its onslaught, we laid there, wiping the sweat from our eyes so we didn't miss anything important.

Even retelling this story, I don't understand why we didn't just go to one of their houses, where the air wasn't 75 percent lava. But then I remember what my house—our home—meant to us. We would rather be miserable there than comfortable anywhere else. So we stayed—and loved every minute of it.

Stuart, Nico, and Joe were as close as any three brothers ever were—and this bonding took place in our home. That summer Nico's mom jokingly offered to pay me for lodging, but we both knew we couldn't pay for what our kids had. It was priceless.

"Build it and they will come" was the message of the great movie *Field of Dreams*. The same can be said of your home. Build it around your kids and make it a warm and inviting place for their friends. When friends become like family, it means more of a good thing. So give your kids another reason to love their home—because that's where their friends are.

Be Part of the Fun

You already know that the demands on your time are as unyielding as they are unlimited. That's our life, and there's no getting around it.

But as important as the work is, so is the play. You need to engage your kids on their level. Be part of their fun—and not only on vacation or day trips but also in their home.

Horsing around with your kids adds a totally new dimension to your relationship with them. It is time they will always cherish, and you will feel the bonds of love tighten when you do.

So don't let the work crowd out the fun. It's too important to both your children and you. It may be only a few minutes a day, with more on the weekend, but don't let too much time pass without laughing with your kids. It's great therapy and has a miraculous-like power to put everything you do into proper perspective.

Remember: the fun doesn't need to be sophisticated or expensive. Simple and spontaneous works just as well, and they are much easier on a lean budget and a tight schedule.

My boys and I played hide-n-seek in the house until they were too big. Then I'd hide Stuart and let the two older boys try to find him. Our family games of Old Maid would become so loud with excitement that we couldn't play in restaurants. And there was nothing like a good water fight. Sometimes, when the kids least expected it, I would execute a preemptive strike.

Stuart loves to tell about one such occasion:

At home it was well understood that there were certain boundaries that one never dared to cross: lying was punishable by death, we were never allowed to start fights but were expected to finish them, and if you were caught failing to address an adult as "Sir" or "Ma'am," you might find yourself sleeping out back with the dogs. Those were the specifics. Everything else could have been summed up as "common sense." Mom knew that we had it—most of the time—and she expected us to use it. Failure to do so usually ended up with a smack upside the head. Which is why I was so surprised one cool summer night when Mama Bear suffered a complete lapse of judgment.

My cousin Anton was visiting us for a couple weeks, which I was ecstatic about because we were like brothers but without the fighting. We had just entered the kitchen to get some snacks and drinks before taking our places on the couch in the den. Through the sliding-glass door that led to the back porch we could see my mom spraying every-thing down with the hose. As we stood there I heard the door slide open. I looked up to see Mom with a look of brilliance on her face, as if she had just discovered cold fusion. She hadn't. She had just found a way to entertain herself. The hose in her hand, pointed straight at us in the house, was evidence of that.

Time stood still. I felt like I was in High Noon, right at the final standoff.

"She wouldn't," I thought to myself. She did.

As the water left the nozzle, Anton and I exploded into motion. We were no rookies to a good old-fashioned water fight, but we were caught off guard.

In our scramble to stay dry, newspapers and bills flew through the air. Mom had lost her mind. Nothing was spared—even the dogs got hit.

After taking cover in the laundry room, with the sound of water hitting the door and my Mom laughing like a mad scientist crossed with a hyena, we managed to make a secret plan.

"Take these and get to the sink," I told Anton as I handed him the dog's water bowls. If I had learned anything from my older brothers, it was that getting even wasn't good enough. We were drenched. So with any luck there would still be some slobber left in the bowls. "You'll know when to strike," I assured him.

As soon as the stream died down we put our plan into action. I went first, to give Anton time to get to the sink. I sprinted for the stairs, headed to the basement, and made my way out back through the sliding-glass door under the porch. Mom's plan was solid, but what she hadn't counted on was how much I had learned from our weekly Western movies. Thanks to the final scene of The Good, the Bad, and the Ugly, *I knew that if you took away the ammo, the gun became useless. Which is why I couldn't help but grin as I finished turning the water valve and felt it seal shut. Mom's surprised shout was music to my ears.*

I made my way back upstairs and grabbed the extra dog bowl from the counter; then we made our charge. Anton went first, but he tried to get too close in an effort to maximize damage, and Mom grabbed the bowl before he could react. He underestimated her—I wouldn't make the same mistake.

With her wrestling Anton for control of the filthy water bowl, she was too distracted to see me—until it was too late. Realizing that she had no hope for escape, she tried every trick in the book.

"Stuart! I'm your mother!" I took one step closer.

"I'm warning you, young man! You will be in SO much trouble!" Another.

"One! Two!"

My brothers and I never knew what happened when she got to three, and we sure as heck never wanted to find out, but at the same time she had always taught me to finish any fight I found myself in. So I did.

The look on her face as the water splashed over her was even more satisfying than the scream that left her lips. Unfortunately victory was hard-won, and she managed to toss Anton's bowl back at us.

I'll never understand what possessed Mom to start that battle, but I suppose I shouldn't be surprised. After all, the apple doesn't fall far from the tree. And I was one stupid apple.

I have no idea what possessed me to take a hose to my kitchen. I only know that when I saw those two kids standing there, so vulnerable, I couldn't resist.

The boys loved it when I went out of character and acted like a kid. And their faces would light up when I pulled up a chair to join their friends and them for a game of cards, charades, or Ping Pong.

To be honest, I should have done it more. It was easy to do and didn't cost anything but time.

Being a mom is so much fun. Don't miss out on the good part just because you're doing it alone. Enjoy your kids. Clown around with them. Make them laugh and give them a chance to make you laugh. Schedule time with the kids and then surprise them with more. These are the moments you will never regret—and your kids will never forget.

The Bottom Line

Homes are powerful places. Inside their walls kids' lives are shaped and their families defined. Give your kids a strong and healthy childhood by making their home a family-centered, magical place to live. Teach them that they're part of something bigger and better than themselves by making them live that way—as a family.

You don't have to fill your home with dogs and cats or even a half-dozen friends for that matter. A parrot, a goldfish, or a dozen clay pigeons might work for you. You and your kids may prefer to eat your popcorn while doing a three thousand–piece puzzle rather than settle in for a night at the movies with John Wayne. You don't have to do it my way, but you do have to do it.

So here's Rule #5: "Give your kids a home to love." Make it a special place for them. There is no better use of your time or greater gift you can give your kids than a good home. But it requires you to set aside family space, drive your kids there, and join them. You and your kids have to live together—talking and laughing, playing and sharing, loving and caring. It's what makes families strong.

Chapter Six

Be Their Parent— Not Their Friend

I used to tell myself that if my firstborn, Billy, didn't turn out well, I had only myself to blame. The Lord had sent me a perfect child. All I needed to do was to keep him that way. Tommy, however, was from a different mold. If he turned out well, I was sure there would be angels singing my praises when I got to heaven.

In my mom's words, "Tommy was born angry." He came to earth with a "Don't bother me and I won't bother you" attitude. I was the exception to this rule, but I'm not certain it had anything to do with me. I just happened to be there when he came to realize that, much to his dismay, he was going to need someone to take care of him. So he looked around, saw me, and thought, "She'll do." That's when he reluctantly let me inside his world and we bonded.

Few others were so fortunate. When visiting the grandparents, my dad would greet him every morning with a big smile and a loud "Good Morning!" Tommy would look him right in the eyes and respond with an equally loud, "NO!" "Nice kid," my dad would say.

Until he was nearly four his public vocabulary consisted of seventeen different versions of the word "momma" along with his favorite word, "no." He didn't need people and learned early to communicate this point, repeating it numerous times if necessary. There was no doubt Tommy was a tough little kid. But he was mine, and I loved his indomitable spirit.

Underneath it all this second son of mine was a good kid. He was just born with my Irish temper and a powerful determination to get his own way. It was a combustible combination—especially for a little guy. Whereas a few strong words or a time-out was all I needed to keep Billy in line, that got me nowhere with his younger brother.

When Tommy would act up, I'd try to send him to his room—he'd refuse to go. So I'd pick him up, and he'd fight to get free. Incredibly strong, he would kick, scream, and grab the stair railing to stop me from putting him in his room. It was one stair at a time and a workout that used every muscle in my body. Finally I'd reach his room, throw him on the bed, and tell him to stay there. Then I'd shut the door as I left. Within seconds that door was open and Tommy was standing there, yelling, "I'm coming out!"

Then one day he did. He came out of his room without permission. He was escalating the battle, and I had had enough. He was four years old and already challenging my authority. I needed to match his determination or I would lose.

I took him back to his bed and spanked his thigh. He hit me back. Shocked at the audacity of this kid, I spanked his thigh again. And he hit me again. This was not going well. And I wasn't about to allow this one-two act continue another round.

I went to my bathroom and picked up my brush—it was one of those with the flat back, almost like a Ping Pong paddle. I returned to his room and gave his thigh one good smack with the backside of that brush. It stung and startled him—and he was furious. Now I had his attention. He took no further action other than to stare at me hard and direct a few choice words my way (something like, "I hate you"). I gave him that, explained he was never to hit me again, and left him there to contemplate the consequences of his actions.

Fifteen minutes later he asked me if he could come out of his room. It was a seminal moment for us. His coup had failed, and I was back in control. Tommy accepted me as his parent with all the rights of authority therein. Or he simply saw that he had one formidable opponent and, for the moment at least, would leave it at that. Either one worked for me.

Over the years I made good use of that brush—not so much to spank a thigh as to threaten to do so. It was all that was necessary. Tommy knew I wouldn't hesitate to use it if he gave me cause, so generally he didn't. But if he came close, I'd give him a little reminder.

Take, for instance, when Tommy was five and wanted to play soccer. I told him he'd have to stay with it the whole season if he joined the team. He agreed. After a few weeks, however, his tune changed. He described the sport as "running around a field after a stupid ball in the hot sun." He then added, "It's dumb and I'm not playing anymore." There was no question in my mind that he had nailed the sport, but I couldn't let him break the rule. He'd made a commitment and needed to learn that those were things you kept. There would be no quitting.

Tommy didn't buy it. His dad took him to the next practice and brought him home early. "He won't play," he told me. I knew differently.

I sat my son down for a little talk, revisited the rule, and explained that whether he liked it or not didn't matter; he had agreed to play out the season when he joined—and that's what he'd do.

His response was all Tommy: "You can't make me play. If you try, I'll walk off the field."

That's when I got the brush out of the bathroom, showed it to him, and let him know it would be in my purse during all his games. If he ever walked off the field, I would spank him right there in front of everyone. The ball was now in his court.

The following Saturday there were two games taking place—the boring one on the field and the one going on inside our two minds. He wanted to win this battle against me as much as quit the team. And

I knew I wouldn't spank him in public—I'd never embarrass him in front of others. But did he know this? (Then there was the little issue that some politically correct parent might call the authorities on me.)

Several times during the game Tommy stared me down and started moving off the field. Each time I pulled the brush out of the purse just enough for him to see. And each time he stopped in his tracks. He finished the game on the field that day, just as he did all the others.

Tommy learned two things that Saturday. First, it was my job to make the rules in our home, and second, it was his job to obey them. That's how it worked. We may have had a crazy home, but I sure as heck was going to run it.

Note: Tommy needed a strong hand to keep him in line, but I could do that and I did. I was his parent and responsible for teaching him to respect authority and obey the rules. He learned fast. By the time he was in kindergarten he was a happy, high-energy child, and though tough, he was a wonderful little boy. And that indomitable spirit of his continues to set him apart from the crowd even today.

Before continuing, let me say a word about spanking—that is, nonabusive corporal punishment to a child's backside or thigh. Some believe the practice should be banned. That's not my take. If time-out worked for all youngsters, these people might have an argument. But it doesn't. I would never have gained control of my second son without spanking. It was an effective and efficient parenting tool that saved this child and me a lot of heartache.

As a parent you have the extraordinary responsibility of teaching your kids right from wrong and good from bad. Your guidance and instructions are critical to them, as is the example you set. They need to know *from you* that all life's choices aren't equal—and that you're there to help them make the right ones.

It's about showing them the way and keeping them on the path. And it's no easy task. It requires an unyielding determination that your children will succeed and an unwavering commitment to do all in your power to assure they do. The first step down this path is to give your kids boundaries. Then enforce them, day after day, until they're all grown up.

You have enormous influence over your kids—far more than anyone else. By setting down rules and putting teeth in them, you show your kids what's important to you. When you stand firm, refusing to compromise, your message is simple and clear: this principle has great value, so much so that I will fight to make it part of who you are.

The reverse is equally true. When you fail to enforce a rule, you're telling your kids that you don't care all that much about this principle. So why should they? Rest assured—they won't.

If kids think for a moment they can pressure you to bend a bit here and there, they'll work you over for days until they get what they want. Tell them what they can't do—and what they must do. Then see to it that they stay within those boundaries.

As a mom—and especially if you're a single one—it is absolutely essential that you establish rules in your home and then enforce them. You can't avoid either step. One simply doesn't work without the other. There's no escaping it. Your kids will have plenty of friends in their life, but only one mom. You need to be their parent, the person in charge—friend doesn't cut it.

Expectations, limits, and enforcement are every bit as vital to your kids as reading and writing. Just talking to them is completely inadequate. In fact, it's nothing but a cop-out. Your kids need absolutes from you, not chit-chat. Give them clearly defined rules, explain the driving principles behind them, and tell them that, as a member of your family, they're expected to live by these rules. Then see to it that they do.

Establish Boundaries and Then Enforce Them

Enforcing rules can be time consuming, confrontational, and emotionally draining. But you still have to do it. And expect your darlings to come a' calling at the worst possible moment—the lowest point of your day. They're pros at timing—and even better at making you feel mean and unfair. When you're thinking "I don't have the energy for this," they're thinking, "I have her right where I want her." Next thing you know you're considering how much easier it would be just to say, "Okay, but just this time." Don't do it. It will only encourage them, and you'll never have peace again.

I found the best way to deal with begging kids was to keep it short. No lengthy discussion. Get right to the point: "You know the rule, so you know the answer." Then add with emphasis: "And that's final." Give them no hope—discourage them from ever coming back. Don't give an inch. Kids are good at this game and have taken down mightier moms than you and me. If you let them talk, they'll wear you thin, and your rules will be reduced to mere suggestions, which will be rejected and discarded at the peril of those you love the most.

In a 2003 *Washington Post* editorial, Sarah Brown, CEO of the National Campaign to Prevent Teen Pregnancy, made the following observation:

> Talking to your kids is absolutely essential. But it is also absolutely insufficient. Two decades of top-notch research—including the widely respected National Longitudinal Study on Adolescent Health, funded by the federal government—clearly show that it is the overall depth and texture of relationships ("connections") between parents and kids that make all the difference. This research also shows that setting fair limits and expectations—and enforcing them—is critical.*

Decades of studies have determined that limits and expectations, clearly established and consistently enforced, are a critical part of parenting. Don't fool yourself into believing you can do less and all will be well. You can talk up a storm and be their best friend, but if there

---

*Sarah Brown, "Just Talking Is Not Enough," *Washington Post,* September 28, 2003.

are no rules to back up the talk and no enforcement to back up the rules, your ability to influence your kids' behavior will dry up one sunny afternoon. Bank on it.

In this same article Brown writes about a friend of hers who raised seven children. Brown asked this mom "what she would do differently if she had it to do all over again." This mom responded that "although she remained a great believer in being an approachable, open mom, willing to talk about all subjects great and small, she said, 'I really wish I had told my children more often what I thought was right, and then tried and make it happen. I was so concerned about being a flexible friend that I sometimes forgot to be a parent.'"

You can't afford to forget to be a parent, especially if you're a single one. There's no one else to pick up the slack. You need to show your kids the way—the right way. You can't be hesitant or shy about guiding them through the first eighteen years of life. The job requires boldness, confidence, and courage. It's all part of being the adult, the boss, or, more simply put, their mom.

Being a parent to your kids—and not their friend—gives order and structure to your home, grounds your kids with a trusty guidebook for life, and builds their self-confidence as they live up to the expectations made of them. You also strengthen their connection to their family, increase the love and comfort they feel in their home, and endear them to you as someone they know is watching out for them, someone who deeply cares for them. What's more, you teach them how to be parents themselves. And that's just the short list!

Take the bull by the horn and be a parent to your kids. Teach them right from wrong by what you do and say. Set the rules to put them on the right path—then enforce them to keep them there.

All Rules Aren't Equal

The goal of rules isn't to control but to teach and guide. So you have to pick and choose wisely. For this reason a closer look at rules in general is warranted. Along the way I'll use a few personal anecdotes to make a point. I hope that from these you'll gain some ideas or insight into what may—or may not—work for your family.

#1. When Kids Are Young, Enforce Rules Only a Few at a Time

When my boys were young, I was determined they would be well behaved, courteous to adults, respectful to others, have superb table manners, and never use bad language—all by the time they were four. I may as well have asked them to fly. Little guys need to be introduced to rules a few at a time. You work with them until they have a grasp of those few, and only then do you add another. Otherwise you're always on their case—instructing and correcting them whenever you're together. That's no fun for anyone. What's more, it adds a boatload of anxiety to your kids' lives, which is the last thing you want to do.

I had to trim back my list of expectations—pick a couple to teach now and get serious about the others later. You will have to do the same. I, for instance, decided that the "No bad language" rule would stay and table manners would be put on hold, which would explain why Billy, as a youngster, was able to entertain his younger brother by splitting his peanut butter crackers in two and plastering them to his head.

When it comes to rules, remember that kids aren't adults. Be patient. Start with the most important and add more when they're ready. Don't expect too much at first. Calmly and kindly repeat, repeat, and repeat. Most kids will pick them up quickly and will want to please you. Others will challenge you. That's when you need to show them who's the boss.

#2. Too Many Rules Are Not Good—
Give Your Kids Some Space to Be Themselves

Don't regulate every moment of your kids' lives. Limit your rules to the important stuff, and give them space to make some decisions on their own. How else will they learn to trust their own judgment? A dress code, for instance, is critical in today's world. It may be as simple as "dress modestly" or "dress appropriately for your age" or both. Or it could be the old common sense rule: "Use your head or you're not getting out the front door in it." Then let your kids choose outfits and dress themselves in accordance with your code.

As young as possible, let your kids have some control over their lives. Although you can't let them break the rules, you can allow them room to move inside the boundaries. Clothes are one way; hair is another. It's one of the places where I gave my kids full range of motion to do anything they wanted. I put all the responsibility for hairstyling into their hands when they were five. What's more, I never second-guessed their decision. Whatever they chose, I respected—that was the rule. Billy threatened a mohawk on a few occasions. I warned him to be prepared—people might laugh, especially his brothers, who were slyly encouraging him down this treacherous path. But I also told him that if this was something he really wanted, he should go for it. He could always cut it off. In spite of my support, he never took the plunge, opting instead for the buzz.

Years later it was Tommy's turn. The summer before high school he and his friends decided to dye their hair blond. I told him I'd help—I bought the dye, put the net on his hair, and, as his friends looked on, I pulled strands through and plastered them with the solution. I was quite impressed with the results, but it was way too subtle for my teenager—he wanted a statement, not a hundred skinny blonde streaks. He retrieved the yucky mess from the trash and smeared it all over his head. His brown hair turned white and orange. It was awful—and he was thrilled.

My friends were aghast that I aided and abetted Tommy with this project. But why not? I had rules against drinking, smoking, drugs, and dating. I even had rules against bad language. He was a teenager looking for a way to be rebellious. I was all there when he chose his hair as the means to that end.

It is easy to get nervous about giving your children a little space. But it is the smart thing to do. They need to become comfortable making decisions for themselves. Whereas I required my boys to play a musical instrument, I let them choose which one. And though I expected them to play a sport every year, they chose the sport. You are their parent, but they are individuals who must learn to pick and choose for themselves within the boundaries you set. Don't micromanage their lives—just instruct and guide them, and then keep them on the right path.

#3. All Rules Aren't Equal

There are rules, and then there are *rules*. They all aren't equal. The ones based on a moral principle, for instance, should be etched in rock and fully enforced throughout the life of your family. Others may need to be tweaked or altered over time, and a few may need to be stricken from the books altogether. Let me give you a few examples.

From my earliest days as a mom I established this family rule: my boys would play both a musical instrument and a sport every year. I was a tone-deaf kid from a tone-deaf family. My three could have been child prodigies, and I'd have been the last to know. But the boys' dad had great musical talent. So I felt lessons were in order. As for sports, I grew up with a coach as a dad and I played three team sports every year from tenth grade through college. It was one of the great joys of my youth, and I knew the life skills that teamwork taught. I also knew that sports kept kids out of trouble. It was all good, so my kids would play.

My plan worked great. Billy chose violin when he was in third grade and played through high school. He picked up piano along the way and sang solo for the church choir when he was twelve. As for sports, he played soccer through grade school, ran cross country and track for his high school all four years, co-captained these teams his senior year, ran in college, and picked up a boatload of medals along the way. Even today Billy runs dozens of miles a week.

Tommy picked the saxophone as his instrument of choice in third grade and played for his grade school orchestra for years. He also took piano lessons for several years, when real talent emerged. When he lost interest in that, I allowed him to move to the guitar. As for sports,

Tommy was a natural. He played soccer, baseball, and football a few seasons each, but his true love was basketball. He played on teams every year from the time he was eight until he was eighteen. After that he found pick-up teams wherever and whenever he could and still plays today.

Then there was Stuart. After years of piano lessons he had the basics down and little more. He wanted to quit every year, but I was determined he would play some instrument right into high school, just like his brothers. After a few more years at the keys, however, I wasn't sure which of us wanted him to stop more. He never seemed to progress, and I couldn't stand the racket. After five years I gave up the battle.

But the kid was a musical genius when compared to his athletic skills. Stuart played on a soccer team when he was six. His games were painful to watch. I couldn't believe he was mine. When I established the "One Sport a Year" rule, I never imagined I would give birth to an athletically challenged child. I gave up all hope of Stuart playing team sports and moved him into Tae Kwon Do. He excelled for about a year—until he advanced to the level that required physical contact. He wanted out, and I didn't blame him. By seventh grade he still couldn't hit the rim with a basketball, couldn't catch a football, and was consistently picked last for any team in his gym class—and kids made fun of him. Who needed this? I took up Stuart's cause and wrote dozens of letters to his teacher to get him excused from gym. *At least he could swim,* I thought—*all was not lost.* Amazingly, in his senior year of high school, he developed into a fine athlete and played rugby for several years. Today Stuart is a first-class basketball coach to eighth graders.

The older boys couldn't believe I didn't make Stuart maintain their high standards. "You're going to wreck that kid," they told me for years. "You need to be as tough on him as you were on us." They were right about one thing: I was the parent they needed when I made them stay with music and sports for all those years. They excelled in both, gained incredible confidence, learned to perform under pressure, and found a lifestyle they loved. I was the immovable object, forcing them to stay the course, and they benefited enormously. The rule worked for them; I saw that every year they lived it. I wasn't going to abandon it just because they wanted to quit from time to time.

But it didn't work for Stuart. I had to accept this and change the rule. It's one of those lessons parents learn on the job: kids aren't all made the same, and the path that's perfect for one doesn't necessarily work for another. They have different strengths and weaknesses, and as their parent you need to help them recognize, appreciate, and develop their particular talents. And your expectations for them, adjusted and revised, should lead them in that direction.

#4. Encourage and Praise Your Children—
It's the Fun Part of Keeping Them on the Right Path
Tell your kids good things. Encourage them, lift them up, and inspire them with your words. Shower them with praise. Let them know how pleased you are with their progress and how proud you are of their good decisions, and congratulate them on their accomplishments. Look for what sets them apart, what makes them special, and draw attention to it—over and over again. Make them feel good about themselves constantly.

Billy, for instance, had this big beautiful smile that could light up rooms. There was power in it, and I wanted him to know he was meant to use it. So I never stopped telling him. Who else would have told him if I had not?

Every child has features that are classic beauty or uniquely interesting. Could be the face, eyes, or hair; could be body type or the stature. Let your kids know what their best traits are. Comment on their clever expressions, funny remarks, great insight, or artistic talent. Let them know how impressed you are with their strength, courage, tenacity, obedience, determination, or hard work. Give them reasons to believe in themselves.

When Stuart was in high school, I worried he was self-conscious about not being an athlete. I searched for ways to assure him that he was still a great kid. Finally one day I approached the subject directly—I wanted to give him a chance to talk about it. "Stuart," I said, "just because you don't play sports doesn't mean you're a . . ." *What an idiot I am*, I thought. *How am I going to get out of this one?*

Stuart came to my rescue. "The word's nerd, Mom, and it's okay. My friends and I are self-proclaimed nerds and we're proud of it." Stuart was completely comfortable with who he was—and no one had better friends than he did. Both were gifts he would carry with him through life. And here I was worried he wasn't athletic. He taught me much that afternoon. His easygoing, witty personality was going to take him far, and I never missed an opportunity to tell him that.

Don't ever let a day go by without saying something good about your kids. Tell them they are the greatest—because to you they are. They need to feel this deep inside, and if they do, they'll be far more likely to respect your rules. So when they choose some wacko outfit with clashing colors, say something positive. You don't have to like their style to appreciate their flair and their courage to go outside the box. So tell them. Build them up. Give them the confidence that comes with knowing they did well.

Your kids should always feel that they don't have to do everything exactly as you would. They are people too and need to be respected as such. You need to support and praise their efforts to be different—as long as it is within the limits you've set.

This lesson smacked me upside the head one evening when Billy was in fifth grade. I found him upside down on his bed reading, a couple books open on the floor and a math notebook on the desk. He explained he had done some of his history reading, had worked on a few math problems, and was now studying English. I couldn't deal with this. I told Billy he needed to work at his desk, take one assignment at a time, complete it, and move to the next. It's how I always did homework, so he needed to do the same. After going a couple rounds with him and getting nowhere, I told him he could do it his way, but if his grades weren't good I'd be back. I left in a huff.

By the time I reached the end of the hall I thought, *What am I doing? What business is it of mine how he studies?* He was doing his homework; just because it wasn't in accordance with my sense of order didn't mean it wasn't done well. When Billy's report card came in, I headed directly to his room. I congratulated him on his exceptional grades and added, "By the way, Billy, study on your head if you like. You'll never again hear any criticism from me."

There are so many ways to be there for your children—and loads of praise has a role in most every one of them. Encourage your kids as they take steps to live up to the expectations set for them. And bury them in praise when they meet the challenge. Uplifting words can be a powerful force for good—make them part of your parenting style.

#5. Prepare Your Kids for the Next Set of Rules

When the boys were little I had no specific rule concerning dating. It wasn't on my radar because it wasn't on theirs. But before any of them were teens I learned that many of my friends didn't allow their kids to date until they were sixteen. I liked this—I liked it a lot. And that's when I did something that saved me years of arguments. I established the "No dating until you're sixteen" rule and repeatedly told them about it long before they cared. By the time they had any interest in the opposite sex this rule was part of our family culture, and group activities became a regular part of their life. In fact, as each of my boys finally turned sixteen, they had grown so accustomed to hanging out with groups of kids that they often chose it over pairing off. One of the smartest things I ever did was prepare my kids for this rule years in advance. Then, when the time came, I had no difficulty enforcing it.

Think ahead: what are the guidelines that may not be relevant today but will become particularly significant when your kids become teenagers? Make life easier for you and them by establishing those rules now. For instance, when, if ever, can your kids pierce their ears, wear makeup, wear heels, date, get a tattoo, get multiple body piercings? Let them know now. Give them a dress code before they care about clothes. Tell them when they're eight years old that no Gothic garb will ever walk out your front door. If you establish the rules of teen behavior early in your home, you give your kids something to look forward to: getting pierced ears and earrings when they're twelve, makeup when they're thirteen, dating when they're sixteen. And it lets them know what's off limits. Most importantly, it gives you control on how—and how fast—your kids grow up.

Don't be afraid to restrict your kids dress, looks, or activities. You are their parent, and it is your responsibility to give them guidelines, keep them on the right path, and teach them the values you want to become part of their lives. Make them aware of the rules they should expect in the future. Then enforce the rules that apply now. When they become teenagers, they'll fully appreciate that uselessness of taking you on—your reputation as The Enforcer will have preceded you, making your job that much easier.

#6. Don't Back Away from Tough Rules—
But Work with Your Kids to Make Those Rules Easier

When the boys were teenagers, I never had to tell them to finish their dinner—they'd have two servings of everything on the table and then go immediately to the refrigerator looking for more. But when they were young, I did have a soft rule about eating their dinner. Often one of them would say he didn't want any more. I'd look at his plate and say something like, "Five more bites." Billy would then eat five more bites. Not Tommy. As mentioned before, the kid didn't like being told what to do. So he would counter, "How about three?" and negotiations would begin. I'd say four and he was happy. The four bites were gone within minutes.

Tommy had to feel he was part of the decision—as if he had won something. So I let him. I'd up the number to eight bites knowing he would counter and after a few rounds we'd agree and both be happy with the results.

Stuart observed all of this for some time when he decided to give it a try. One evening when he was about six he indicated he didn't want any more of his dinner. I told him he had to eat five more bites. He countered, "How about eight?" *Kid takes after his dad,* I thought, and quickly sealed the deal.

Although there was never any softening of the "No dating until you're sixteen" rule, I gave them an alternative—group activities—and then I worked with them to make it happen. Generally that meant driving. Whether the group was going to the ice-skating rink, the movies, or a dance, I was always available to take, pick up, or do both. I did whatever was necessary to see that they enjoyed the company of young women as long as it was within the guidelines I had set.

Then there was the "No beach week" rule. This is a high school tradition in which the seniors designated a week and a beach and then encouraged their classmates to get together, rent accommodations, and go unsupervised. I saw it as a twenty-four-hour, week-long party during which nothing good ever happened. So my boys would never experience it—not as long as I was alive.

Tommy, however, was determined to go. He was eighteen, had graduated from high school that morning, and was going away to college in three months. That was his argument and it had some merit—but not enough.

"But all my friends were going," he pleaded. Whatever possessed the kid to think that extraneous bit of information was going to get him anywhere was beyond me. I explained that his friends didn't have a mom named Bay—but he did. And what's more, "You're not going."

That night he went to a graduation party and ran into the father of a boy who desperately wanted Tommy to be part of his group at the beach. When my son explained to this dad he couldn't go, his friend's father told Tommy, "I'll call your mom and let her know everything will be fine. She'll let you go." Tommy came home with some hope—but not much. He knew me better than that.

"My friend's dad is going to call you," he advised me. "He wants to assure you that everything will be fine at beach week." I thought, *was this some sort of joke? Some dad I had never met thought he could tell me what was best for my son?* The audacity of the man was amazing!

Later that night he called. He told me he was a lawyer or something—like that mattered—and that the kids would all be staying in his beach apartment. Again, the relevance was lost on me. I asked,

"Will you be at the beach with the boys?" Adult supervision might have made a difference to me, but probably not if it was this guy. "No," he said. "But I'd be just a phone call away." What a ridiculous comment—this conversation was full of them. "A phone call away? What good is that?" I asked. "The calls come in after the trouble."

I explained to this dad that we had a rule in our home called, "No beach week"—and Tommy still lived there. So it applied to him.

Some of what Tommy wanted wasn't a bad thing—to hang out with his friends one last time before college. So I made that happen. I had already taken a rental place in Myrtle Beach—two weeks after any beach week I knew of—and told him he could have as many friends as he wanted. I'd pick up the tab and he'd have a different sort of beach week, one where I'd be a lot closer than a phone call away.

Good thing too. I got two calls at the rental that week from the Myrtle Beach police. Apparently a few of Tommy's buddies couldn't avoid a good fight, and the police had tossed them into a holding cell and would only release them to the "responsible party." *Just be happy it's not one of your own*, I kept thinking as I drove into town to retrieve the ruffians. Tommy spent the week corralling his pals and keeping Stuart and his friends from getting near any brawls. I remained nearby reading a novel, waiting for another call, and feeling more convinced than ever that nothing good ever happens at beach week.

———

Don't change your rules to conform to the latest fashions, cultural trends, or the advice of others. They aren't responsible for your children—you are. Don't be afraid of having higher or more stringent standards in your home than those in friends' homes. And never be afraid to be different.

You're a parent—it is for you to decide what's best for your kids. Draw the boundaries, set the limits—and impose the consequences. Care enough for your kids to make the tough decisions for them, and love them enough to enforce them. They can blame you for their modest clothes or no dating rule—it might make it easier for them when they're with their friends. But always explain the principle behind the standards you're requiring. Don't let the culture teach them right from the wrong—they need better than that from you.

And when they find the rules tough going, there is nothing wrong with lending a hand. Try to find an alternative; show them how they might do it within the boundaries you've set. If they don't like your suggestion—fine. But the rules stay in place. More often than not they'll want to work with you—and will ask for help again. But most importantly, they'll learn to respect you as their parent.

#7. Let the Consequences Be Known

Whenever possible, attach a punishment to your rules. Let your kids know in advance what the consequences are. It will often serve as an effective deterrent, and when it doesn't, enforcement will be so much easier. What could be clearer to a five-year-old than "I'll clean your mouth out with soap if you say bad words" or "See this brush? I'll not hesitate to put it to good use if you come off that field."

When it came to my brothers, my dad found that pulling the keys to the car was a most effective consequence. So when Mom asked that he not confront them about their hippy looks when they came home from college for the holidays, he agreed. Instead he met them at the front door with a new rule: "No one with hair below their ears will be allowed to drive any of my cars." Worked every time. I'd be called into service that same day to cut their hair within a fraction of their ears. The car was more important than the hair.

Dad used the same enforcement method on my youngest brother, Tom. One summer when he was in high school Dad asked him to weed under the bushes on both sides of our long driveway. It needed to be done by the weekend or Tom wasn't driving anywhere. Early Friday evening Tom learned his friends couldn't drive—if he wanted to go out he needed to get access to the car. Knowing there was no negotiating with Dad, Tom grabbed some gardening tools along with a flashlight and headed out for a few hours of night weeding.

That evening I had a date with a new guy—someone who had never been to my home. It was dark when he arrived, and he couldn't see the street numbers. So he parked and went to a neighbor's house, where he was directed to ours. Rather than get back into his car, he decided to walk up our long driveway to pick me up.

Meanwhile, using his flashlight to see, Tom was totally focused on weeding the bushes. Out of nowhere he suddenly hears footsteps and realizes someone is right up on him. Frightened he jumped out of the bushes, put his flashlight into the intruder's face, and demanded, "Who are you? What do you want?"

My date, whose heart had completely stopped, sputtered, "I'm looking for Bay Buchanan." This odd person whom he knew only as the man in the bushes with a flashlight let him pass.

When my date and I walked down the drive, I spoke briefly to my kid brother. Once safely in his car the fellow asked, "Who is that guy?" "My brother," I answered. "Your brother?" my date said incredulously. "What the devil is he doing in the bushes?" "Weeding," I explained. There was nothing more I could say.

Dad got his bushes weeded, Tom got the car, and I lost any chance of ever seeing that guy again.

There was no negotiating with my dad. We did what he asked or we paid the price. It saved both of us a lot of time, eliminated all the theatrics and begging, and earned him our greatest respect. It was a lesson I learned young and carried with me into my own years of parenting. As a single mom of three highly charged boys, it was one of the wisest things I ever did.

Kids need to be taught that there are consequences to their actions. It's an invaluable lesson that can change the course of their lives. Teach them young and repeat it often. Disciplining your children promptly and consistently will reinforce the message that they have to pay a price for wrong choices—and it will keep them from running you ragged. Choose punishments that are effective, not excessive. You want your kids to expect what is coming, to know it is fair, and to accept it when it happens.

Even with Rules, There Will Be
Troubled Waters and Stormy Seas

My kids were born strong willed, high spirited, and packed full of energy. They were all boy. But even knowing this I was still alarmed at the amount of trouble they got into, even as youngsters. It was a sure sign of times to come.

One evening my neighbor came to our door to complain that Billy was destroying his flowers. Billy denied any involvement. The next day I happened to come home early and caught the kid finishing off the remaining blooms. He had his little brother in tow—showing him how it was done. They were four and two.

On a walk home from kindergarten, five-year-old Tommy, in response to a dare from his little buddies, threw a rock through the back window of a brand new van parked along the way. His friends complimented the little vandal on his arm.

When Stuart was seven, a little neighborhood friend was at our home playing. Bored, Stuart went into the garage, picked up an ax, and chased the kid home with it. We never saw the kid again—but I did get a call from his mother.

There was ample evidence that these three were going to give me a run for my money. But for some inexplicable reason I would occasionally be overtaken by a sense that my boys had moved to the next stage of life, that a maturity had taken place—and they had emerged as responsible young people. It was sheer lunacy; I should have never let my guard down with these kids—at least not with the younger two. They would prove me a fool every time.

One such occasion occurred when my oldest entered his teens. I kept thinking about what was important to my brothers at that age and remembered how often they spoke, with near reverence, of their BB guns. And that's what occupied my mind as Christmas approached that particular year. I'll let Stuart take it from here.

People make mistakes. Everyone does, so when it happens, it's rarely some big occurrence. That's not the case with Mom, though. You see, she rarely made mistakes, so those few times when it actually happened, it could be classified as a disaster. One such catastrophe involved Tommy, me, and a pair of BB guns.

If you've ever seen the movie A Christmas Story, *then you already know that a ten-year-old and a BB gun is a proven recipe for disaster. Lucky for us, Mom had never seen it.*

It all started with a holiday trip to Sports Authority. One of us kids spotted them a mile away—to be honest, I wouldn't be surprised if we had actually sensed them before they were even in sight. As we drew closer I swear there was a heavenly spotlight outlining their magnificence. Almost on cue, all three of us turned, mouths wide, and stared at Mom, trying to speak but settling for telepathic shouts. "WE HAVE TO HAVE THESE." I don't remember what her response was, but if I were a betting man, I would say it was something along the lines of a laugh, followed by a firm "Do I look dumb?"

Mom always entertained a small measure of pleading before making her final decision. Come to think of it, that is probably how she made her decisions. If we begged hard enough, she knew it was important. If we gave up right away, then she knew we didn't really care. Needless to say, in front of that glorious stand of pristinely packaged Red Ryder BB Guns, we put on an Oscar-worthy performance. Our efforts were not appreciated.

Defeated, it was off to Toys R Us, where we distracted ourselves by choosing our next battles—LEGOs, action figures, and video games. Mom was always very generous at Christmastime.

When Christmas morning finally came around, we all gathered around the less-than-ideally ornamented tree and sat as patiently as three young boys can be expected to sit when there is a horde of treasure within arm's reach. After setting up the ground rules (we had to take turns; battle royales were frowned upon on Christmas Day), Mom gave the okay and we went to town. When all was said and done, and we all had big grins on our faces, Mom pulled out the big guns. Literally.

While we were distracted and drooling over our awesome acquisitions, Mom slipped out unnoticed. She came back with three of the most beautifully wrapped, perfectly large boxes we had ever seen. We set a world record with how fast we tore those presents open. We could not have imagined how incredible the contents were. It was a Christmas miracle that none of us dropped dead just at the sight of them: three Red Ryder BB guns.

Super Bowl championship celebrations cannot compare to the noise we made that morning with our crisp, new rifles in hand. In mere seconds we had them loaded and were out the door, without a care in the world that it was freezing outside and we were still in our pajamas. Mom shouted after us, "Don't ever point them at each other!" Unfortunately for her rule, nothing in the world could distract us from our joy in that moment. Well, except for competition.

Billy was old enough at that point to be responsible with his gun. Tommy and I, however, were anything but.

It could not have been more than a few weeks before trouble started brewing. Tommy and I would spend afternoons in the tree house out back, taking turns with a little target practice. As always, things deteriorated quickly, and Mom's rules were promptly thrown out the window.

Although I don't remember exactly how it started, knowing Tommy and me, I'm sure he said something that got my blood boiling. I decided to get even by taking aim at his dog, Spike. In my defense, Spike was more bear than dog, and he had chased me around the backyard so many times that he had this coming to him.

Well, as any ten-year-old is apt to do, I failed to think my master plan through. Tommy let out a flippant "oh yeah?" and put my dog, Nicky, in his sights.

How dare he? Who does he think he is, threatening my dog? I'll show him. This train of thought was followed by me pointing my rifle straight at Tommy's head. The look on his face almost made up for the retribution wrought by my mother's hand. I will never understand how she always knew when we were about to do something especially stupid, even by our standards. Was it a sixth sense? And did she have some hi-tech device that determined both our exact location as well as the most effective trajectory for her hand to do the most damage to our heads?

But this time, no sixth sense was needed. Tommy, never failing to seize an opportunity to get his little bro in trouble, saw Mom through the kitchen window, where she was busy washing dishes. He took aim and fired. After the distant "tink" from the BB hitting the window, Mom looked around the kitchen with a puzzled look on her face. Tommy pumped his rifle and fired again. This time she looked directly at us, and her previously puzzled face now wore a new and much more terrifying expression.

She came out onto the porch in such a fury that I thought her mere anger would bring the whole tree house down around us. Needless to say, we lost all BB gun privileges for a while.

Mom made an uncharacteristically large mistake when she bought us those guns. Her second mistake was giving them back to us.

Shortly after the dog-threatening episode, Tommy and I were out front practicing our aim yet again. We thought it would be a grand idea to take shots at the lights on the front porch, and we were both proud of our skill when we managed to shoot out the glass panes covering our respective targets. But it was cold out still, and after a while I was ready to go inside. Tommy, however, had to be the one to decide when it was time to quit, and he made that quite clear when he put my head in line with his sights.

Never one to miss an opportunity to get my brother in trouble, I shouted "Mom" at the top of my lungs and took off for the front door. Luckily for me, a Red Ryder BB gun takes a twelve-year-old about two minutes to load and pump. I made it safely inside and began to taunt my brother from the other side of the glass door. Tommy's only response was a distinct ping as a BB hit the door—and embedded into it.

My jaw dropped. I ran into the kitchen to show Mom just how dumb my brother really was as Billy came down the stairs. Upon seeing the BB's effect on the glass door, Billy let out a "whoa." As I tried to explain to Mom what happened—being the first one to do that was important, as a little spin could go a long way—Billy's dumbfounded cries grew louder and clearer: "Whoa, WHOA, WHOA," CRASH. Mom and I ran into the hall as the entire glass door shattered into a million tiny pieces and fell to the ground. Tommy stood on the other side of the empty space where a door had been just seconds before. Then came the reckoning, and what a glorious reckoning it was. For me and Billy, that is. I'm sure Tommy remembers it differently.

I don't know what I was thinking giving those two boys BB guns. I knew better.

My boys fought one another at home, classmates at school, and strangers when the opportunity presented itself. I had multiple appearances before principals, headmasters, and deans of students. These three handsome young men totaled four cars, were involved in a dozen lesser accidents, and were required to explain their driving habits before judges a half-dozen times. Life was never dull around our home.

But the rules remained in place. And when they broke them, they paid the consequences. I didn't always succeed, but I never stopped trying. My boys meant everything to me; they were my family and I believed in them. No matter what happened, no matter how difficult the challenge, I never doubted my kids could make it. And I knew my job was to do all in my power to see that they did. So when they came up short, I swallowed my disappointment, reminded myself they were kids, and turned all my energies on getting them back on track. It was during these times that I grew closest to my boys—and when I saw in them their greatest strengths.

It is easy to get discouraged, to feel the struggle is too great, to become overwhelmed by the setbacks. But your kids aren't perfect. Like mine, they're going to bring home bad marks, problems with teachers, and stories of falling out with friends—and they're going to make bad decisions. This is when they need you the most. Always find the time to have a serious discussion with your kids or to give them a strong dose of encouragement. Maybe a listening ear is all that is called for—but even that requires a few quiet minutes of your time.

Expect your kids to make mistakes—and expect a few of your own. It's part of life. It doesn't matter how good a parent you are—these two things are going to happen. So when they do, don't get down. Get tougher. Dig in deeper. Be more adamant than ever that they'll make it—and then guide them past their troubles and back onto the path you have set for them. Your kids need to know that you will always be there for them—not just cheering from the sidelines when they do well but also by their side when they fall.

The Homework Grind

In fifth grade Tommy went to the front of his class to collect a test paper that he was required to have me sign. On top of the page was a big red "C." He turned, faced the class, and said, "Everyone, I want to say goodbye. When my mom sees this, she's going to kill me."

When he told me about his little theater at my expense, I was surprised he appreciated how upset I'd be with his lousy mark. My boys generally did well in school—at least in those early years. There was no need to say much about grades. Even without a specific rule, Tommy understood what was expected. I worked with them on homework, helped them study for tests, and was ready to teach them what they failed to understand in class. There was no reason for a bad grade in my home—except laziness.

That evening I explained it to Tommy this way: "If God gave you a C brain, I would be happy with C's. But he gave you an A brain. So get A's. Get it?" I didn't need to give them any more reason than that. They had the ability and the support—and if needed, I'd give them a more persuasive argument. That's when Tommy began practicing my signature.

Even with a steady hand at the helm, kids have a mind of their own. Once high school hit, my younger two found other interests, and I had to settle for an ever-increasing number of C's. But I never gave up on their grades—always giving them—or finding them—help to keep them from getting behind. Then when they finally realized how important it was to their future, they were in a position to do well on their own.

Parental expectations and involvement are the most significant factors in a child's academic success. You must throw yourself into the homework grind. Make your kids show you their work; see that it is complete. Review test material and read their papers. Ask them every day about specific classes and then listen to their responses. Don't hesitate to call a teacher to confirm. Keep yourself fully aware of what's happening in their classrooms. There is no better prevention of academic problems.

Too many working moms are leaving schoolwork entirely up to their kids. Oh, they may ask them at night if all their homework is done. If they get a positive response, they're relieved and consider their job done. But kids are more than capable of telling you what you want to hear—especially if they know you aren't following up on them. You can trust them all you want—but verify. Double- and triple-check that your kids are on top of their schoolwork. Don't let them get behind. It doesn't matter how busy or tired you are at night; you need to see to it that your children have all the tools they need to succeed and that they are using them effectively. Let your kids know what you expect. Tell them that, with their abilities and hard work as well as your support and guidance, they can do it. Don't let being a single parent be an excuse for your kids to perform poorly in school. Be tough and demanding when it comes to their academic success—their path in life depends on it.

The Bottom Line

I have read accounts of parents who feel they shouldn't tell their kids not to use marijuana. The quasi-logic goes something like this: they smoked it when they were younger, so they feel that forbidding their kids to do so now would be hypocritical. These folks are living proof that marijuana adversely affects brain cells. The fact that you may have broken important rules some time in your life in no way eliminates your responsibility to teach your kids to do better. You are the adult in this relationship—you need to act like one.

Hollywood and the music industry glamorize adultery and promiscuity while fashion designers push provocative and immodest styles on young people. The Internet puts pornography a button away, and alcohol and drugs are easily accessible. Being a young person these days is tough—it's hard for them to stay out of trouble. As a single mom you are a one-person army against a powerful, all-present, wayward culture. But don't think for a moment you don't have a chance. You are perfectly positioned to influence the decisions your kids make and the people they become.

Use your authority as their parent to guide your children through the minefields. Set the limits, teach the principles, and enforce the rules that'll keep your kids on the path you've determined to be the safest, healthiest, and wisest route for them to travel. Be absolute in your convictions of what is right and what is wrong. Let your kids see and feel the certainty and confidence with which you speak. Be clear, firm, and bold when you talk to them about your expectations of their behavior.

Set their standards high and never drop them. Don't let style trends determine what your kids wear—give them a dress code. Don't let modern culture be their guide—enforce your rules. Don't let friends influence your kids more than you—be a parent. And always remember that your kids can't do it without you. They are going to need to lean on you to live up to the standards you set, so be steady, be strong, and be brave—be the mom they need.

You are the boss, the adult, the parent. You are not the friend. Good parenting requires consistent and fair enforcement of established rules—and single parenting demands it. If you want your kids to succeed, you have to be an actively involved parent who is immovable when it comes to keeping your kids in line.

Love and discipline is what good parenting is all about. With rules, kids thrive; without them, they get lost. Do what is best for your kids. Make expectations and rules part of your family, and give these rules and expectations meaning by enforcing them. It's Rule #6: "Be their parent, not their friend—set rules and enforce them." It may be tough, but it is what kids need—and what you will do if they are first in your life.

Chapter Seven

Create the Magic of Great Family Traditions

A friend of mine, a college professor, became a single dad nine years ago when his wife died. He was left to care for his three teenage daughters and an eleven-year-old son. His grief drained him of energy, and by the time he left work he was exhausted. But his day was long from over. Every night when he walked through his front door, he came face to face with the brutal reality of being solely responsible for raising his children.

He had no idea how he was going to keep his family moving forward, to help them deal with this terrible tragedy and show them how to get on with their lives. He didn't even know where to begin. Both a counselor and a good friend suggested he start by simply having dinner with his kids as often as possible. He didn't know how to cook or what his kids liked to eat, but he had to do something—and this was as a good a place to start as any. So he gave it a try.

This highly educated single dad had no idea just how great a starting place he'd stumbled upon.

Before she died his wife gave him some recipes. He also called a friend to get a few more, the kind with no more than three ingredients and could be ready in twenty minutes. It wasn't a time for complicated meals with obscure ingredients; he was just looking for a passing grade.

Then he told his kids he needed their help. He wanted to have family dinners but didn't know how to go about it. They decided they would gather in the kitchen every night at six o'clock. Some would help cook, others just hang out. But they would be there together, cooking and eating, talking and laughing, and catching up with one another—as a family.

The six o'clock dinner hour became a tradition in his home, one that anchored his kids and him during tough times, helped each of them heal, and comforted them with the knowledge that even though their mom was no longer with them, they were still family. Sometimes the meal time lasted only twenty minutes; other times they talked around the table for hours. Either way it was time they came to count on to reconnect.

As the years passed, my friend's kids grew closer to him and to one another because this single dad established a family tradition of eating dinner together. In addition this simple practice fueled many more ideas for family time that further bonded his family.

Today he lives alone—his kids are married or away at college. But when the holidays come around, you can find this professor in some kitchen alongside his son cooking the turkey (their responsibility, his son tells him) with his daughters nearby. It's their tradition.

———

There is nothing like traditions. Packed with incredible power, as my professor friend learned, they can slowly transform a group of individuals, struggling to find their way, into a strong, close, highly functional family. The magic lies in their ability to influence the attitudes, behavior, and choices of those who participate in them.

Family traditions are the most powerful tools you have in your possession. There is nothing that works as well to guide and direct your family. Why? Because family traditions give your kids roots that ground them and a structure that stabilizes them. Your kids physically see and emotionally feel an undeniable attachment to their family—creating within each of them that invaluable sense of belonging to something bigger than themselves.

Traditions establish a familiar but special world for your kids. This is their life—it's what they do and who they are. They grow comfortable with the routine and secure in their role. The traditions you choose for your family will define the culture in which your kids are raised, give direction to their lives, and leave them with precious memories that will last a lifetime.

Most family traditions are simple, reoccurring practices in which the family participates together—family habits, if you like, like family dinners, evenings, and vacations. To succeed, some must be compulsory—as the parent, you have to require attendance. Others will be welcomed activities. But to be effective you have to define them, establish them, and participate along with all your kids. They don't work without you.

I was raised in a family rich in traditions. We ate as a family, went on vacations together, went to the same Catholic grade school; my seven brothers went to the same all-boys Jesuit high school, and my sister and I attended its sister school. All of us attended church on Sundays, and every brother was an altar boy. These traditions defined the kind of family we were, instilled in us a traditional set of values, and played a significant role in making each of us the people we became.

It is up to you to decide what your family traditions will be. Some folks speak two languages in their home, others celebrate more than one set of religious holidays, and then there are those musically talented families that regularly sing and play instruments together. These are all great traditions that add texture and character to your kids' lives. Others use more basic activities—such as puzzle making, camping trips, or, my favorite, movies—to create time to be together with their children. There are scores of possibilities from which you can choose—some from your own childhood, others from friends, and maybe a few that are original to you.

No matter how many traditions your family enjoys, however, there are two that must be part of the mix. Why? Because over a decade and a half of studies prove that these two traditions have an incredibly powerful influence on the healthy development of children.

They are family dinners and family attendance at weekly religious services, and they may well be the most effective parenting tools available to you. Although at first they may be difficult to establish in your home, you still have to do it because, working as a pair, these traditions will strengthen your family as nothing else you can do.

We'll examine more closely these two important practices. You'll see that it is impossible to exaggerate the benefits to your kids that family dinners and attending church together will provide. We'll also look at several other traditions that work wonders as well.

Eat Dinner Together as a Family

After sixteen years of studying teen behavior, the founder and chairman of the National Center on Addiction and Substance Abuse (CASA), Joseph Califano, concluded, "Simply put: frequent family dinners make a difference."

Their studies have "consistently found that the more often children have dinners with their parents, the less likely they are to smoke, drink or use drugs, and that parental engagement fostered around the dinner table is one of the most potent tools to help parents raise healthy, drug-free children." *

More specifically, their 2010 report on family dinners found that "compared to teens who have frequent family dinners (five to seven per week), those who have infrequent family dinners (fewer than three per week) are

- Twice as likely to use tobacco;
- Nearly twice as likely to use alcohol; and
- One and a half times likelier to use marijuana."

---

*The National Center on Addiction and Substance Abuse at Columbia University, "Accompanying Statement by Joseph A. Califano, Jr. on the Importance of Family Dinners VI Report," September 2010, http://www.casacolumbia.org/templates/ChairmanStatements.aspx?articleid=607&zoneid=31, paragraph 2.

Imagine! By simply eating dinner with your kids five to seven evenings a week, you can dramatically reduce the possibility that your kids will smoke, drink, or use drugs! And it doesn't stop there.

A Minnesota study, published in *Archives of Pediatric and Adolescent Medicine,* found that "teenage girls who ate five or more family meals per week were less likely to resort to extreme dieting measures like using diet pills or laxatives, binge eating, and vomiting to control their weight. The results suggest that encouraging family meals may be an effective way to combat the growing problem of eating disorders among teenage girls."

So what are you waiting for?

If you don't have a rock-solid routine of eating dinner with your kids, start today. (I told you dating won't work!) There is no time to waste. Make family meals mandatory for you and your kids. Tell them, "Six o' clock, in the kitchen, with me—every night." This guarantees a daily time slot for you to reconnect with your kids—to review their day, talk through issues, and just touch base with them. By listening to them and observing them every night, you will be able to sense problems, influence decisions, show them you care, and be the parent your children need.

And your kids will love it—even the teenagers. According to CASA, "Teens themselves understand the value of family dinners: nearly three-quarters of teens think that eating dinner together with their parents is important. Most teens (60 percent) who have dinner with their parents fewer than five nights a week wish they could eat dinner with their parents more often."

If family dinners are difficult for you to organize, then delegate. Pass some of the responsibility onto your kids—setting the table, making the salad, cooking the meal on Monday and Wednesdays, or cleaning up afterward. If your kids are anything like mine, though, you probably want to do it all yourself. Remember: simple, easy meals work—order in pizza or pick up Chinese if time is tight. It's not what you eat—it's the conversation, the catching up, the care and concern that goes on while you munch down your food that makes the difference.

And if your job makes it impossible to have family dinners, do the next best thing. Have family breakfasts. Get your kids up a half-hour earlier in the morning and use this extra time to eat with your kids, review their day, and talk to them. Let them see every day that they belong to a family and that you are always there for them. Then pack your weekends full of family meals and start looking for another job. You need to be eating dinner with your kids at least five times a week.

Single parents can least afford to pass up the amazing benefits that come with family dinners. It is critical for your kids. It's what they want—and what they need—because if you aren't with them for this meal, they're eating dinner without a parent, day in and day out. Where's the family in that?

The evidence is undeniable. Family dinners work wonders. There can be no more important time for you to be with your kids. Sitting around the same table every night talking and laughing creates a powerful sense of attachment to one another. Children see and feel that this is where they belong—at this table, in this home, and with these people. And therein lies the magic. It should be no surprise that this results in children with far fewer problems.

Four Ways to Get the Kids Talking at the Dinner Table

Family dinners were a central part of my life as a youngster and played a critical role in making me who I am today.

At age six I graduated from the "kids' table" to the "big table," and nearly every night for the next twelve years I ate dinner sitting in the same seat. It was my place, on Mom's immediate right. At 6 p.m. nine of us would stand in front of our designated places and wait for Dad and Mom to join us. Then after Dad blessed the food, we sat and began our meal.

During these family gatherings I learned what my siblings were up to; heard stories about aunts, uncles, and grandparents; and listened to my brothers and my dad debate religion, politics, and sports—an exercise that invariably deteriorated into outright arguments. But this was my family and it was here—at this loud and boisterous dinner table—that I became curious, confident, and conservative. It is where I learned to tell stories, laugh out loud, and hold my own. And it is where I developed my love for God, family, and country.

I knew what family dinners had meant to me, and I wanted the same for my boys. But there was no dad at my table, no stay-at-home mom, and certainly no amazing meal. It was just the basics—a parent who had worked all day and then raced through traffic to get home and sit with three boys who showed no interest in my presence. The only thing my dinners appeared to have in common with those of my youth was the prayer.

I admit: I struggled with these dinners. With only one adult at the table, conversations tended to fall into one of two categories: kid-to-kid and kid-to-boring parent. My boys preferred the former. I can't blame them. They spoke to one another with great animation, responded to comments with lightning speed and laughed continually. I understood nothing. When I asked what they were talking about, they would fire off a few words in my direction—"new computer game" or "TV show"—and then immediately re-engage with their brothers.

I did try. I would ask some version of "Anything interesting happen today?" Nope—Nope—Nope. Three kids—three Nopes. There was one evening, however, when Tommy broke this tedious routine and reported, "My teacher threw a kid out the window." "What?!" I yelled. "Why?!" "Bad kid—drove the teacher crazy. He landed in the bushes." Just the bare facts—no more. All four of us laughed hysterically—and yes, the teacher was fired.

My boys volunteered little information about their lives. They controlled the dialogue and chose to talk, joke, tease, and laugh among themselves. I was reduced to the status of an observer. But even then something good was happening. My kids loved one another's company, and family dinners deepened their relationships as nothing else I did.

But this wasn't enough for me—I wanted more of a presence at these meals. So I came up with a number of ways to make that happen.

1. Ask Specific Questions

I changed my approach—no more generic questions for me. Those were getting me nowhere. I started using more specific queries to draw them out. I'd ask how they did on the math test, if they got their English paper back yet, or when basketball tryouts were. I became a machine—asking questions, following up, and cross-examining. I was a parent on a mission; I wanted to know what they were doing and how they were doing, and this daily hour was perfectly positioned to get me that information.

2. Discuss the News

I began to introduce a news item—something I wanted them to know. I never missed an opportunity, for instance, of telling them about some poor kid who, after playing a computer game nonstop for forty hours, collapsed dead of a heart attack. And yes, this could happen to you, I assured them. Or when there was a trashy story about Dennis Rodman—a sports hero of Tommy's—I introduced it for discussion. It was an excellent opportunity to let my kids know that one's personal life is far more important than their athletic abilities. Then to prove my point I banned all Rodman paraphernalia from our home—including the poster in Tommy's bedroom.

I read the paper every day, and once I began looking for them, I always found articles I could use to drive a conversation at dinner.

3. Tell a Story

I'd tell stories—about relatives, about when the kids were younger, about me, and about people in the news. If I came across a funny news story, I would throw it out at dinner. I loved to see my kids laugh, and I loved laughing with them. And once we got started there was so much back and forth—it became a family affair. After a while the kids would come to the table and say, "Mom, I have a story," and with all eyes on them they'd hold forth and entertain their family. This became as much a tradition in our home as the dinners themselves. Even today the boys will call me and say, "Hey, Mom, I have a story."

4. Play a Game

When all else failed, we'd play games—something the boys always loved. Family favorites were multiplication and square root problems or crossword puzzles. I'd call out the problem, and whoever answered first won the round. This pastime was good for as long as I was willing.

And when I caught them bickering, I'd make each of them say good things about their brothers. I was hoping to hear a little appreciation for one another's finer qualities, but it never quite worked out that way. Instead Billy would say, "I like Stuart's shirt" and "Tommy plays a great game of basketball." But even that broke the tension, and as other ridiculous comments followed, the boys all would start laughing—so it did the job.

Dinner hour was hard work for me, but I was determined to get my kids talking to me. I wanted them to know what I believed, what I valued, and what I expected of them. So I talked, I asked, and I listened while I sat at our dinner table with my boys. By the time they were teenagers the boys took my interrogative style in stride. They came to understand it was just what their mom did—and I used this to my full advantage.

As a teenager, my second son, Tommy, was my biggest worry. When I spoke to him about his less-than-stellar grades, he would explain, "Billy spends his week studying, Mom. I spend my week planning the weekend." There was no guile in the kid. But I knew I best keep a close eye on him—and there was no better place to do it than at the dinner table. Midweek I'd ask him about his weekend plans. The next evening I'd follow up. I wanted details—vagueness put me on high alert. When his friends came over I'd ask them—always looking for inconsistencies.

They told Tommy, "Your mom sure asks a lot of questions." And I wasn't stopping anytime soon. I wanted Tommy and his buddies to know that they had at least one parent watching their every move.

Family dinners can be a chore for all moms. But for single parents it can be downright painful. Without another adult at the table this tradition can turn into a mind-numbing kiddy hour. Don't let that happen in your home. With a little imagination and a lot of determination you can—and must—make dinner the most important time you spend with your kids. You've set it aside—now make it work for all of you, not just the kids. Use family dinners to engage your kids, to laugh with them, and to guide them. Remember: it's the family interaction that releases the magic.

Attend Church as a Family

"Religion can benefit your children immeasurably," so says CASA's Joe Califano after researching teens for over a decade and a half. I saw this as a youth, believed it as an adult, and wanted it as a mom. But making it a tradition in my home was more difficult than I ever imagined—and more worthwhile than I ever dreamed.

At 11 a.m. every Sunday morning for the better part of twenty-five years, my dad could be found climbing the first half of the attic stairs to wake my brothers. "Pat, Jim, get up," he would yell. "The last Mass is in forty-five minutes. Get up and get ready for church."

Most of my brothers slept in the attic bedrooms, and Dad would wait on those steps until he heard movement. If it didn't come, he'd begin all over again. "Pat! Jim! Get up now." The only thing that changed over all those years was the names. As the older boys left home the younger ones became the focus of his attention. It didn't matter how old they were, what time they got home, or how badly their heads hurt. It was Sunday morning, and what mattered to Dad was that his kids went to church. And as long as they lived under his roof he made certain of it.

Attending church on Sundays was important to Dad, and by making it mandatory he made it a habit—one that lasted a lifetime—for all nine of his kids. Though I converted to Mormonism in my twenties, I continued the practice. Going to church was an integral part of my life, and I had every intention of doing so as a family when the time came. But once again single parenting turned this great tradition into a painful ordeal for me, so much so that I gave thought to abandoning it—at least until the kids were older.

It was on a blistering hot September morning and I was six months pregnant with Stuart. I was in church with Billy and Tommy—they were four and two years old, respectively. They began to fight and, within minutes, were throwing punches. I couldn't pick up Tommy because of the pregnancy. So I grabbed them both by an arm and dragged them out of church and into the awful heat. Physically tired and emotionally drained, I didn't know if I could keep this up.

I spent every Sunday morning getting myself and my kids ready for church, packing bags of diapers, toys, books, and snacks. Then I spent over an hour in a chapel trying to keep them at arm's length. With the number of kids soon to be three, all I could see for years into the future was week after week of Buchanan family fights inside the sacred house.

To make matters worse, attending church as a single mom was emotionally brutal. They were unbearably lonely hours. Though I managed to keep these feelings under wrap throughout the week, they overwhelmed me as I sat alone in church with my boys. It wasn't the way it was supposed to be—and I felt the enormity of the loss. The time I spent in church was the toughest and saddest hour of my week.

And for what purpose, I thought. As distracted as I was and discouraged as I felt, how could it possibly be good for me? How could I possibly expect to gain strength by putting myself though this ordeal every Sunday? And the kids didn't seem to be benefitting much either. At least that's how I saw things that hot September day.

I admit that I had my share of "Woe is me—I am a single parent" moments, and this was definitely one of them. In reality I was looking for an excuse to make life easier for myself—at the expense of my kids. I knew the incredible strength my siblings and I drew from having religion in our lives. I wanted the same for my boys. Question was: would I fight like my dad to see that it happened?

It was only with unrelenting determination that Dad was able to make church attendance a tradition in his home. I could do no less. Especially since I knew what Dad could never have known—the extent of blessings that would flow into his family as a result. Surely with this knowledge I could find the same kind of resolve my dad had.

So I gave myself a week or two to feel sorry for myself, and then, for the sake of my kids, I made an absolute commitment to attend church every Sunday as a family. It didn't matter how trying it was for me—or them. It was where we belonged.

I taught my boys that this was one of those rules etched in stone. They had no choice in the matter: as long as they lived in my home they went to church with their brothers and me. At some stage during their teen years each of the younger two informed me they weren't going anymore. They were old enough to make this decision for themselves, they said, and what's more, I couldn't make them go. The revolts failed within minutes—apparently they weren't ready to move out of the house.

Get Your Kids Actively Involved in Their Church

As they grew into young boys I realized it shouldn't stop with church on Sunday. These boys needed to be active members of their church—to understand what it was to be fully involved in their faith. I required them to attend youth activities and service projects. In high school I made them go to church outings and youth camps in the summer as well as seminary during the school year—a religion class held at 6 a.m. on weekdays. They would fight me, of course, but I never backed down. How could I? They came home from the summer programs so full of life, so absolutely thrilled with their experience, and so happy to be alive. Admittedly, the predawn seminary classes were a tougher sell, but by the time they were in high school I needed to throw every positive experience their way in hopes of keeping them on the right path.

Take Tommy, for instance. He had a heavy beard at fifteen, was lifting weights at sixteen, was bulking up by seventeen, and all the while thinking about girls. He was an all-American kid—good looking and confident. He came to church with a two-day beard and baggy pants, but always with the required white shirt and tie. And he didn't just walk into church: he shuffled, dragging his shoes, with shoulders slumped under the heavy weight of the attitude he carried. No one in that church doubted that this kid was present only under duress. But he was there, every Sunday, sitting with his family—and that's what mattered to me. Something good could happen as long as he was where he was supposed to be. I was certain of it.

The summer after Tommy graduated from high school—the same month I refused to let him go to beach week—I told him I had signed him up, along with his kid brother, for a week of EFY (short for Especially For Youth). It was a church camp held on a college campus several hours south of our home. I knew if I let him drive he would drop Stuart off and head back home; so I drove the two of them.

At eighteen Tommy was pushing the age limit—and I was pushing my luck. He looked about twenty-five and was months away from the college experience—and I had enrolled him in a summer youth camp with his fifteen-year-old brother. But I put my foot down and he went.

We showed up at camp, where we encountered about sixty kids, none of whom reached Tommy's chin. The female counselors at the registration table began whispering among themselves about the big kid in the line, the one that looked like a college jock. Then they gave him a small wristband with his name on it. Tommy was begging me to let him come home when, out of nowhere, this gorgeous girl comes running up to him and gives him a huge hug. She was a church friend and asked Tommy if he was dropping Stuart off. He mumbled something about his mom signing him up to attend and she said, "It's okay, you can hang out with the other counselors and me." Things were looking up for Tommy and for me.

As I drove away I couldn't stop laughing. It was a combination of the image of him standing with those little kids and the relief I felt having pulled this off. I knew I was asking a lot of this kid, but at the same time I wasn't giving up on him. He was undecided about life. But I had an advantage on him: I was certain of the path he should take and willing to fight to get him on it. But time was running out, and my only hope was to keep putting him in good places so good things could happen.

At the end of the week Tommy called to arrange for a pick-up time the following day. I braced myself and asked how his week was. To my utmost amazement he said it was one of the most fantastic weeks of his life. He told me he never felt so good about his religion and that he wanted to go on a two-year mission for his church. Parental moments don't get better than that.

Once back home Tommy again vacillated between two worlds, but after about six months the message of youth camp won out and this tough kid's life was changed forever.

As do most teenagers, my boys made their share of bad decisions. And as most teenagers, they would never have gone to church if I hadn't required it—with the possible exception of Billy. But by making religion a significant part of their lives I wrapped my boys in a second family—one with teachers, advisers, camp counselors, and good friends. Many of these church leaders played critical roles when my boys found themselves in rough waters, and they were always exceptional role models for them. My kids grew to love these men and women and wanted to be like them. I put my boys in good places— and good things happened.

Ultimately all three of my boys volunteered to serve two-year missions for their church. Billy went to Texas, Tommy to Chile, and Stuart to Italy. There was no coming home, no computer games, and no dating. They spent all their time and energy working with other missionaries in the service of others. Each one of them found the experience to be the most challenging and the most rewarding of their lives. They loved their missions and remain actively involved in their church today.

All this was made possible because one hot September afternoon twenty-some years ago I committed to a simple tradition—weekly church attendance as a family. It was the best decision I ever made as a single parent.

Studies have found that "teens who consider religion to be an important part of their lives are far less likely to smoke, drink, or use drugs."* That's just the half of it. Making your kids part of a church family—regardless of what your faith may be—grounds your kids with a sense of order and direction. It reinforces your message of what is right and wrong and emboldens them to make good decisions and avoid bad ones.

Weekly church attendance with your kids is an invaluable tool for a single mom. It doesn't take two parents for this tradition to work its magic in your family. As the man said, "Religion can benefit your children immeasurably." Make a commitment to consistently attend religious services with your kids—all it takes is a few hours every weekend, but there's no better way for you or your kids to spend that time. Etch this tradition in stone and give your family the transforming power of religion in their lives.

Go on Family Vacations

In Chapter 3 I wrote about vacations as a superb opportunity to be together with your kids. I introduce them again here—this time as a wonderfully magical family tradition. But not all vacations are equal— and it's not the destination or the cost that matters. Rather, it's the quality of the time you set aside to spend with your kids.

---

*Joseph A. Califano, *How to Raise a Drug-Free Kid: The Straight Dope for Parents* (New York: Fireside Div of Simon & Shuster, 2009), 16.

A few years ago I was on a biking trek at the base of the Grand Tetons in Wyoming. One morning as I was making my way around a sharp curve on a wonderfully flat path, a little girl—maybe six years old—came at me from the other direction. She had trouble managing the curve and nearly ran smack into me. A minute or two later her younger brother appeared. He was riding slowly but in complete control thanks to his training wheels. Then, some distance later, I spotted their dad—he was biking along while deeply engrossed in conversation on his cell phone.

These young kids needed their dad to be part of their experience. But he was too far back to talk to them, encourage them, or laugh with them. They deserved better.

Maybe this father spent all afternoon playing with his kids—I hope so. But if what I saw was any indication of his commitment to vacationing with his kids, he missed a precious opportunity to strengthen his family and build memories for his kids.

If family dinners can have a dramatic influence on your kids' lives, imagine the booster shot family vacations can give them—the whole family together, and not just for a meal but for days at a time. You're away from work, the kids are away from school and friends, and all of you are away from cell phones, computers, iPads, televisions, and electronic games. Right?

If your vacation goal is to be engaged as a family, you have to ban or dramatically restrict the use of anti-family toys—theirs and yours. Establish this rule when the kids are young so they never question it. But if it's too late for that, then start now—and be tough. Don't let electronic devices rob your family of precious time together.

Family vacations are one of the most pleasurable experiences you can have with your kids. You all benefit. Relaxing, playing, laughing, and eating together in a new environment for days at a time will remind you just how much you love them. And your kids will get you all to themselves. Create great memories for your kids of time together as a family.

Here are a few thoughts from Stuart on our family vacations:

When I look at the memories I share with my mom and brothers, I see summers full of vacations. Some were better than others, but the important thing is that they're all there, in the back of my mind, waiting to be remembered.

When it came to planning vacations, Mom had a formula that she followed, and after the first couple uses my brothers and I had it figured out. She was dead-set on "culturing" us, as she so subtly put it, which typically meant visits to historical sites or seeing a play onstage. Unfortunately for us kids, the only thing more boring than being "cultured" was Mom explaining it. At our young age, unless her plan included the words "putt-putt" or "waterslide," we weren't interested. But Mom knew us better than we knew ourselves—and planned accordingly. For putting up with her terrible ideas (terrible to a ten-year-old—now I see the wisdom of her ways), we were re-warded with unlimited fun for the remainder of the vacation, which never disappointed. For example, one vacation we went to Williams-burg, Virginia. The culturing took place at historical Jamestown, where we were forced to learn (and later quizzed on) the story of the early American colonists. Once Mom had decided we were one step further from barbarism, we spent the rest of the time at Busch Gar-dens, a nearby amusement park. Mom was crafty, but then again, she had to be.

To say that ours was (and still is) a competitive family would win Understatement of the Year, hands down. With this in mind, let me tell you about an important lesson I learned from my brother Tommy.

Mom, my brothers, and I went to a small family-fun center close to where we were staying. It was your typical attraction: mini-golf, batting cages, and, of course, a go-kart track. Us kids ran over to the go-karts first, as we were too little to use the batting cages, and had already finished more games of mini-golf in our lifetimes than Tiger Woods has played eighteen holes. Much to my horror, even on my tip-toes I still missed the height requirement. Billy and Tommy laughed and hopped into their fun-machines while I clung, distraught, to my mother's side. As the miniature racecars sped (if you can call 15 mph "speeding") around the track, my brothers' competitive spirits kicked in, and to any spectator the scene was indistinguishable from the chariot race of Ben Hur. Mocking, ramming, and likely more than a little cursing certainly made for an entertaining event. But all good things come to an end. Well, unless you're my brother Tommy.

When it came time to end the race, the teenage attendant made the announcement over the PA system for everyone to slow down and then stepped out onto the track as each go-kart came to a stop. And then Tommy came ripping around the corner, approaching the finish line. Mom always jokes that Tommy's first word, and the one used more than any others since, was "no." And not just "no"—it was more like "NO!" I don't presume to know what was going through my brother's head at that moment, but when the attendant stepped out in front of him with his arms wide, signaling him to stop, I imagine it was something along the lines of "NO!"

As Tommy got closer and closer to the finish line and the waiting attendant, it was apparent to everyone in the crowd that he had no intention of stopping. In fact, he actually sped up, although Mom and I could not have known that at the time, because for us, slow motion took over the scene. I don't remember which happened first or if they all happened at the same time. Mom uttered, "Oh, no," under her breath. My jaw dropped as the attendant dove out of the way—and I am not embellishing or taking any liberties with the story here, he literally had to dive—just in time to avoid the embarrassing injuries associated with getting run over by a ten-year-old in a go-kart. Tommy's accomplished grin as he narrowly missed bulldozing a teenaged go-kart track attendant is forever freeze-framed in my memory.

As Tommy sped down the racetrack one more time, being pursued by words I dare not repeat for fear of having a bar of soup shoved into my mouth, I thought to myself, "Unless he plans to get all the way to Mexico in that thing, he's a goner." When the now-sweaty and tired attendant came back to the crowd, he demanded, in no uncertain terms, to know who that [insert profanity here] kid's parents *were, at which point I looked up at my mom, who grabbed my hand and whispered, "Let's go, Sweetie," and we slowly faded away from the crowd. Pretending that we had no idea who Tommy was remains to this day as the single greatest game I ever played as a child, and I like to imagine that I was quite good at it.*

On-the-spot corrections were the only time Mom ever saw fit to punish us in front of others, including each other, so I never knew what happened to Tommy once she got a hold of him. I do know that he survived the exchange, which was a miracle in and of itself. But I did learn a valuable lesson that day: sometimes it's best to just stay out of the way. So thank you, foul-mouthed go-kart track attendant, wherever you may be.

Memories of family vacations are some of our finest. It was prime time for the four of us. We grew closer on every one of these adventures, and my boys became best friends all over again. It's what made these trips so special for me. These were indeed the best of times.

As a single mom you need to vacation with your kids. Time away from the distractions of home, school, and work is sweet time for all of you. You don't want to miss this or the benefits that come with it.

Have a Weekly "Family Evening"

Your kids need lots of family time—it is what makes their world secure and happy. But once your kids are in school and engaged in extracurricular activities, time together can get lost in the craziness of schedules. That's why you need to designate blocks of time every week to spend with your kids—and not just for family dinners and church attendance. You also need to put time aside just to be a family—a weekly family evening. It is another powerful parenting tool.

I tried to incorporate this tradition in our home when the boys were young. My church encouraged it for all parents, suggesting that Monday night be designated as family night. The idea was simple enough: parents and their children should put aside every Monday evening for some family activity—could be board games, storytelling, or a talent show. You might include a discussion or a teaching moment. Or you may turn the time into a meeting with the kids to review the family budget, chore assignments, and upcoming events.

I tried Monday night, but it was too tough. My workday evenings were packed with the endless demands of three boys. My family nights were sporadic at best. So I changed the night to Friday, when I knew I would be home with the boys and ready to relax. I thought, *why not make it special time?* To assure that I would enjoy these few hours as much as the kids, I designated it "movie night" and made it a family tradition. Every Friday evening we would gather in the den with pizza, smoothies, and unlimited popcorn to watch a movie. It was the best night of the week.

Before they were ten my boys had most John Wayne movies memorized—they were family favorites for years. When Tommy was eighteen, he met and took out a really cute girl. When he came home, I asked him how it went. He told me he couldn't go out with her again. "Why not?" I asked. "Mom, how can I date her?" he asked me in all seriousness. "She doesn't even know who John Wayne is." He had a point.

This great tradition turned us into a movie family—we watched them, talked about them, and played games with their titles. We even extended the tradition to Christmas and Thanksgiving evenings. We would go to one of my siblings' home for dinner—I wanted the boys to spend these holidays with their cousins—but after the meal we would head to the movie theater as a family. We all looked forward to it; not only were new movies usually out, but we also had the theater virtually to ourselves.

Turn a Child's Important Events into Family Affairs

There's another family tradition that I established in my home that is worth mentioning because it played a significant role in teaching my kids that there were obligations associated with being a member of a family. I wanted my boys to be close, and I was willing to go to great lengths to make it happen. I needed to know they would be there for each other if something happened to me—and this would only happen if they cared deeply for one another. When they fought, I'd tell them, "just remember—he is going to be your best friend one day." They would scream in horror at the thought, but I was convinced that if I constantly worked at it, I could create brotherly bonds that would be nearly unbreakable. And if I succeeded at that, my boys would indeed be best friends for life.

So I made certain that not only did my kids do things together but that they also were aware of what was happening in one another's life. Along these lines I made them attend all major events in their brothers' lives. I went to nearly every one of Billy's cross-country meets and talked about them at our family dinners. But when it came to his championship race, the brothers attended as well. Likewise, I went to most of Tommy's basketball games and would relive them at our dinner table. But we went as a family to his championship games. And when Stuart won his gold medal at the Tae Kwon Do championships, we were all there.

We went as a family to music recitals, graduations, and award ceremonies. I wanted my boys to actually be part of their brothers lives— not just individuals living under the same roof. I felt it was important they saw their brothers doing what they did well—and support them doing it. Don't get me wrong. The boys groaned when I told them about a sibling's Saturday night recital. But that didn't stop me from making them go. They needed to see what set their brothers apart from others so they could more fully appreciate them. And they needed to learn what it meant to be part of a family.

When Stuart was in college, he played on his school's rugby team, and one Saturday they traveled to Provo, Utah, for a game. He must have texted his brother Billy, who lived in the area, that he was coming to town. Without my knowledge Billy and his wife went to see him play. Afterward Billy called to tell me about it—and let me know Stuart really was good. I had such a rush of joy. Billy got it—he was there to support his brother. It was a beautiful thing, and it has happened many times over. Traditions work.

The Bottom Line

One of the most difficult aspects of being a mom is that there is too much to do and too little time to do it. You spend so much of your time and energy just keeping the balls in the air that you can lose sight of your principal goal—to tightly wrap your kids in the love and security of a strong family.

This is why traditions are invaluable: they make family time routine. They guarantee that you will give your kids what they need the most—time with you. There is no substitute for it. It is by your side that they can see your commitment and feel your love. It is only together with their family that they can grow close, attached, and secure.

The evidence can be seen in the traditions of family dinner and church attendance: they are powerfully effective parenting tools with "immeasurable" benefits for your kids. These traditions are gifts to single parents—difficult at first to organize, but once they're a routine part of your family's life, the rewards are incalculable.

As one single mom to another: do right by your kids—eat with them, go to church with them, and establish other family traditions that bring all of you together in a special way every day of the week. There is no time to waste. Release the magic that's in Rule #7: "Establish family traditions—make time with your kids' routine in your home."

Chapter Eight

Love Being
Your Kids' Mom

Billy, my oldest, began talking at the age of two. Nothing particularly noteworthy here except that he skipped the cute baby-speak phase, preferring perfectly formed and accurately punctuated paragraphs that invariably ended with a question mark. This child asked questions all day long. Before he was born I dreamed of having such a wonderfully inquisitive kid. After he arrived I worked to get him to stop—to somehow suppress his curiosity—at least for an afternoon.

It began with the proverbial "Why?" but rapidly grew into an entire repertoire of different lines of questioning. One of his favorite themes was the animal kingdom. "If an elephant fought a bear, who would win?" or "If a lion fought a puma, who would win?" He was relentless. At first I tried to figure it out—no easy task for someone with little to no knowledge of or interest in the subject.

I'd answer "bear" and he'd say, "Why?

I'd tell him these animals don't fight each other and he'd respond, "But what if they did?"

I'd try, "I don't know" and he'd follow with "But what do you think?"

There was no way out. So I did what I promised myself I'd never do—I made up answers and defended them with made-up facts. He drove me to it.

As he grew more mature, so did his questioning. At age four, for instance, he asked me where pee came from. Now this was real life and deserved a responsible answer.

Using an empty glass of orange juice from the kitchen table, I asked him, "You remember the orange juice you drank at breakfast? Well, it went down into your stomach, where your body took all the good parts for itself, and what was left over was passed through your system and came out as pee." He was satisfied and I was happy. I didn't have to decide which ran faster, a giraffe or an antelope.

A few months later the boys and I were at the beach with my parents. My dad had a routine: every morning he quietly ate breakfast while reading the paper. One day Billy and I joined him. Dad gave no signal whatsoever that he was interested in a discussion of any kind— a subtlety lost on Billy, who had spotted the orange juice next to Dad's plate. He asked, "Grandpa, do you know what your orange juice is going to turn into?"

Oh no, I thought, *don't go there.* Dad never talked about "private matters." I tried to head Billy off, but the kid would not be distracted.

Dad turned to him, and using Mom's nickname for my son, he kindly said, "What, Billy B?"

Billy said, "It's going to go into your stomach, Grandpa, and come out as pee."

Dad took one look at the kid, glanced at me, pushed his untouched glass of orange juice some distance from his plate, and returned to what had been a pleasant morning.

———

There is nothing like kids. They're the most entertaining people alive. You couldn't script the things they do and say—and wouldn't want to, because most of it's at your expense. But what's a little embarrassment? It only lasts a short while. But a good laugh stays around for a lifetime.

I've never had more fun than I did being a single mom, nor have I ever done anything more rewarding—not even close. I can't imagine a more fulfilling life. Though painfully challenging and brutally difficult at times, it was twenty full years of excitement and adventure that felt good and right as I lived them and fill me with joy as I remember them.

As I look back I see that as I worked to mold them, my kids molded me. I was constantly stretched to do more, be better, and aim higher. As a mom I learned to stand by my boys, fight for my family, and love unconditionally. My pride was beaten out of me, my priorities cleaned up and straightened out, and my understanding of life infinitely expanded. My years as a mother made me a more caring, more compassionate, and an infinitely more patient human being.

These boys of mine so completed my life that, over the years, I have often felt bad for their dad—what irreplaceable moments he missed with his sons while he was alive. What a heartbreaking loss it was for him not to have known these fine young men as I did, not to have seen how hard they struggled nor how well they succeeded.

Appreciate all that you have—kids who love you, a home full of family, years packed with great memories. It's a good life, so live it right and enjoy it to its fullest. Let your kids see how much you love your life with them. Let them know how grateful you are to be their mom, how proud you are to call them your own. Tell them how your heart fills with joy every time you see them smile, hear them laugh, or watch them sleep.

As tough as it is to do it alone, raising kids is the best job you'll ever have—and the most important. Don't let it slip by without feeling the overwhelming joy that is yours if you do it right. Be the mom your kids need and enjoy the amazing adventure that follows.

I'd like to tell a few stories that are close to my heart. They will give you some idea of just how inspiring kids can be, how they can enrich your life immeasurably, and how much fun life with them can be if you just give it a chance.

I Taught My Boys to Fight

I was raised by a dad who was adamant that his sons know how to fight. He knew from his own life that boys needed to be able to defend themselves, and he was going to make certain his could. And he wasted no time doing it. At age six my older brothers were required to "hit the bag" ten minutes a day. A punching bag hung in the basement, and Dad was there to help with form. Whenever Mom expressed some concern, he'd explain that he was instructing his sons "Never to start a fight—but always finish it."

It's a good thing he did too because, when they were teenagers, my brothers were out "defending themselves" nearly every weekend. At least that's what they told Dad when the police called. I often wondered if maybe the "never start a fight" part of Dad's creed was exclusively for Mom's ears.

One way or the other, Dad taught his boys how to fight. And along the way I absorbed the lesson.

Years later, when my son Billy was about six, he came home from school and told me some kids were pushing him around and knocking him down. I knew just what to do—I had learned from the best.

Billy begged me to call the school and make them stop. I told him I couldn't; he had to solve this problem himself or they'd never stop. Bullies are everywhere, I explained, I couldn't protect him from them. He had to learn to do that himself. It was tough for this little boy, but I assured him that I'd show him how to do it. I would teach him to fight. And while I was at it I'd teach his younger brother too.

Though Billy was reluctant, Tommy was pumped. (What was I thinking? He was four years old!)

I got down on the ground and had them take turns jumping on top of me. I told them to hit me. We did a few rounds of this to give them a feel for a fight. Then I explained they were wasting their energy. They needed to focus their attention on the nose. "Don't bother with the stomach or chest—go for the nose! A good shot there will end the fight fast," I explained. "It will make the nose bleed, and the eyes water—and that's game over." It was a lesson right out of Dad's game book.

They took turns practicing. When it was Billy's turn, Tommy would scream, "My turn, Mom, my turn" as he jumped up and down. Billy, a born pacifist, was hesitant.

"What if I get in trouble for fighting?" he asked.

"Tell them you didn't start it," I said, "that you were defending yourself."

"What if I still get in trouble?" he asked.

"Tell them I told you to do it. I'll handle it from there," I assured him.

He still wanted me to call the school to make them stop. But that wasn't happening. Again I explained that he had to stand up to the little bullies if he wanted them to stop. It was the only way.

For weeks I would come home from work and ask Billy if anything had happened at school, if anyone had bothered him. I knew if he'd just defend himself this once, take these guys on, he'd gain confidence. He'd learn he could take care of himself. But he was a good kid and afraid of getting in trouble. So he either ignored or avoided his antagonists.

Then one day when I picked him up at school, he said, "I did what you said, Mom. I hit 'em in the nose."

I was beside myself with excitement. I told him to hold on a few minutes. We'd go to Taco Bell, sit, eat, and celebrate as he told his story—every single detail of it.

Once he got settled with his taco he began.

"Mom, they kept bugging me and pushing me. Finally I couldn't take it anymore. So I pushed back—until we were up against the wall."

"And then what happened?" I asked.

"I did what you said, Mom. I hit 'em right in the nose."

"Excellent, Billy! That's just excellent! What happened next?"

"Her nose began to bleed and she started crying."

"SHE?? SHE??!!!" I was in shock. He had beat up a girl, and it was all my fault. Granddad would be rolling over in his grave. It was rule number one in our home and the only reason I survived to maturity: you never hit a girl.

Then I remembered something.

"So Billy," I asked as calmly as possible, "what did you tell your teachers?"

"I told them that you told me to do it."

I let Billy know how really proud I was that he had found the courage to defend himself. Then I explained that I had overlooked a point when I taught him to fight. Girls were off limits, I told him. He could never hit one again—no matter what.

There was only one more thing for me to do. I waited for the call from his headmaster. That explanation was going to be a bit more difficult.

And My Boys Fought for Me

After my less-than-impressive performance as a boxing coach, I hung up my gloves. I had taught my boys the basics. It was all I knew, but it turned out to be all they needed.

One day, when Tommy was in fifth grade, he came home and told me to expect a call from the school. He explained he'd been in a fight. When I asked him what had happened, he said a kid had bad-mouthed me. It was during one of those ridiculous insult exchanges kids often got into. One says something like, "You're ugly," and the other says, "You're uglier." Well, somewhere along the line the other kid switched it up to "Your mother is ugly." Tommy decked him. One shot to the nose and the fight was over.

When I heard the details I said, "Good for you, Tommy. I'll handle the call."

I know, I know. I should have added something about self-control and tolerance. But I never told you I did everything right, did I? And between you and me, I figured the little stinker got what he deserved.

A few years later I became cohost of a political program and could be seen on television every weeknight. A few of the kids in Tommy's class picked up on it and every so often took to mimicking me. That was a mistake that always ended the same way—a bloodied nose. Tommy tolerated no disrespect of his mother. His classmates learned not to go there with him—unless they were in a fighting mood. His granddad would have been proud, but no one was prouder than his mom.

My Boys Got Me into Trouble

I'm a big believer in kids learning to swim young, and I had mine taking lessons at the local gym by the time they were three. One afternoon I was poolside watching Billy pass some level of swimming expertise; Tommy had just passed his. Angel, Tommy's best friend, was with us, as was Stuart. Tommy asked if he could show Angel the handball courts inside the complex. The observation window was just down the hall, and we often stopped there to watch a game on our way out. Where was the harm? "Sure," I said. "And Stuart can go as well—just keep a close eye on him." Then they left.

While Billy swam and I relaxed, Tommy took a quick look at the handball courts and found nothing of interest. Then he spotted the emergency door. He led his posse through that door and onto the building's flat gravel roof. That's when he saw the twenty-five-foot ladder that would take them to the roof on top of the elevated section of the gym. By the time the man working in the adjacent office building looked up from his desk, Tommy was nearing the top of the ladder, with Angel close behind him and my three-year-old just a few rungs from the bottom. Stuart found climbing difficult when you're hugging a security blanket.

In total panic the responsible citizen called the gym, and the manager raced to investigate. He couldn't believe his eyes—two little boys and a toddler playing on the gym's roof. A few minutes later—he needed to give Tommy and Angel time to climb down—he came ripping into the pool area, boys in tow, looking for me. To say he was angry doesn't do the man justice. He described all that happened, all that could have happened, and then added something about reckless disregard for the safety of children.

What could I say? He had a point.

Before he left he advised me never to let those kids out of my sight again.

I stared at Tommy in total disbelief, trying to figure out what had possessed the kid. He looked up at me and said, "Mom, I almost made it to the top!" It took this kid less than ten minutes to put himself, his brother, and his friend in mortal danger—and get me profiled as a criminally delinquent parent—and all he had to say in his defense was, "Mom, I almost made it to the top!" It was going to be a long life.

They Made Me Look So Bad

Then there was our summer vacation at Sky Top Lodge. Located on a summit in the Pocono Mountains in Pennsylvania, this old resort had a huge lake, hiking trails, a golf course, and loads of activities. The boys and I had been there the summer before, and I decided we'd go again. We invited Billy's friend Derek to join us. He was Pam's son. Billy and he were twelve.

We left our Virginia home at the crack of dawn. Before heading to the Poconos I wanted to squeeze in a few hours in Philadelphia's renovated historic area and expose my boys to a little American heritage. As a result we didn't arrive at the Lodge until late afternoon.

There was a great waterfall surrounded by huge rocks about two miles from our cottage, and Billy was anxious to show it to Derek. The trail to get there was a wide, well-traveled dirt road, so they could bike most the way. When it became too steep, they would push their bikes. The trip home was all downhill—a fun, bumpy bike ride to a paved path that took you around the lake and right to our front door. It was a favorite spot of ours, and I knew it would take them no more than twenty minutes to get to there and less to get home.

I told Billy not to take too long; I wanted to unpack and then get dinner together. An hour and a half after they left there was no sign of Billy and Derek, so I asked Tommy to get on his bike and find them. I was hungry, and the dinner hour would be over soon. While Tommy was gone, there was a knock on our door. Stuart opened it and screamed for me.

I came around the corner and saw Billy standing there, white as a sheet and covered in dirt. One foot was bare, blood covered his leg, and his right arm hung awkwardly. Stuart headed for the bathroom and locked himself in; it was more than he could handle.

Fearing his friend was in worse shape, I immediately asked Billy where Derek was. "He should be here," Billy yelled. "He left to get me help hours ago. When he didn't come back I got myself free and walked here."

I sat him down, put a pillow in his lap and put his arm on it. I didn't need a doctor to tell me it was broken. I called the front desk and explained that I had one kid who needed medical attention and another who was lost. The lady on the phone asked, "Didn't you just check in?"

What did she want me to say, "Two hours ago—plenty of time to break some bones and lose a kid"?

I turned my attention to Billy and asked him what happened.

He and Derek were climbing the rocks around the waterfall, which were covered with small trees and shrubbery. He was some twenty feet up when he lost his footing and fell. A branch caught him halfway down, but his foot became lodged in a small crevice and he couldn't free himself with one arm out of commission. That's when Derek went for help.

As I learned later, Derek drove his bike as fast as he could down the path. The area was new to him, and his mind was focused on Billy. So he didn't notice the fork in the trail, and instead of going right, he went left. The path he took was an old utility road no longer in use and heavily overgrown. He followed it down a hill and deep into the woods. When his bike could no longer plow through the underbrush, he realized something was wrong. He turned around, but he couldn't see any trail. He left his bike and started walking—deeper into the woods.

While Derek was gone, Billy slowly worked to free his foot. Once on the ground he took off his shoe and soaked his sock to clean the blood off his leg to see how deep the wound was. When no one came to help, he began walking to the cottage. He was in shock. He left his shoe behind for the two-mile trek, and when he came across some hikers, he never said a word.

The resort's security personnel came to our cottage, listened to Billy's story, and immediately put together a team to search for Derek. When they found his bike, they called in the local volunteer firemen to join them. Nightfall was fast approaching, they explained; if Derek wasn't found soon, they would have to call off the search until morning.

The paramedics arrived, put Billy's arm in a sling, and told me he was in shock and they needed to get him to a hospital. I would have to follow them to authorize treatment. I told them no; I wasn't going anywhere. I couldn't. I couldn't go to the hospital with my son and leave Pam's in the woods. I had to know Derek was okay.

I paced outside the cottage. I needed air to think clearly, and I couldn't watch Billy suffer another minute. As I prayed they would find Derek soon, Stuart came out of the house to be with me. He went right to the heart of the matter: "Are you going to call Pam, Mom?" he timidly asked. I turned toward him and yelled, "And tell her what? That I lost her only child in the mountains?" The pressure was getting the better of me.

Back to Derek: after walking awhile he came across an old hunting cabin deep in the woods. It had a fence enclosing its front yard, where the owner's dogs resided. Their angry barks kept Derek from the front door, and when a man inside screamed at him to get away, he left. He wandered around the woods for another hour when he saw a light and followed it. He was back at the cabin. This time when the man yelled, he yelled back that he was lost. It was now dark and he was ready to sleep in the woods if this guy didn't help him. The man asked where he was staying and Derek told him the Lodge.

One quick call later and a couple firemen were on their way to Derek. The next call was to me. Derek had been found, they told me; go to the hospital—we'll send someone to stay with your other kids. Billy was put in the ambulance and I followed. Once there I placed a call to Pam. After two hours of excruciating anguish, I was able to tell her all was well.

This was more than enough excitement for any vacation, but why did I expect it to stop there? The next day, with Billy's right arm in a cast, I told the kids to stay close to the cottage. Late in the afternoon, Stuart, who had only recently mastered the bicycle, was having a blast riding his bike down a hill and onto a practice putting green. He wasn't afraid of falling because he was on grass, and he felt great pride in his accomplishment.

Tommy decided to join him. After a trip or two down the hill Tommy criticized Stuart's conquest as lame. Stuart grew angry and dared Tommy to go down a far steeper hill on the opposite side of the green. A challenge—it was all Tommy needed to hear. He came down the first hill and, picking up steam, headed for the next. What Stuart failed to mention was that this second hill was not only steep, but it also ended in a ditch with a large drainage pipe in it. In fairness, none of this would have stopped the kid—Tommy was under the spell of a challenge. He impressively survived the second hill when his front tire got caught in the drainage ditch. He somersaulted into the air, landed on the road, and his bike came down on top of him.

Within the hour I was headed back to the hospital.

I took a seat opposite a woman whose job it was to register my son as a patient. Tommy was leaning up against me. I explained that he may have broken his right arm. She looked at me, paused, and then said accusingly, "You were here last night with him. Where is his cast?" I told her that was another child. She looked at Tommy, then back at me, and angrily said, "Look lady, I registered you last night and this is the same kid. What happened to his cast?"

I told myself to keep cool; do not react. I didn't need to add the police and social services to this vacation. I calmly commented that my two oldest boys did look a lot alike. "Lots of people say that," I told her and laughed nervously. I then explained that Tommy's older brother, the one with a cast, was back at the resort with a babysitter. "So how did this one get hurt?" she asked incredulously.

All week I prayed that there would be no more trips to the emergency room. Obviously, I didn't want any of the boys to get hurt. But equally important, I needed to avoid charges of child endangerment. It would put a real damper on my ability to make a living.

Here I was, a single mom, taking her kids and one of their friends on a vacation. And within two days I am suspected of physically abusing my kids. I thought about these boys of mine. I thought about what they were capable of. Then I looked in the yellow pages to find another hospital—just in case.

And They Drove Me to the Edge

My job was to establish the rules. I sometimes wondered if the kids' job was to test them. Stuart recounts the state of affairs at my home after I left Tommy alone on a Friday evening:

> *I was recently asked if my brothers and I got into trouble a lot as kids. Once I had recovered from my fit of laughter, I asked the person if bears pooped in the woods. We were kids—getting into trouble was what we did best. During high school I think I spent more time being grounded than not. And seeing my brothers get in trouble gave me more joy than an ice-cold lemonade on a scorching day spent outside weeding Mom's accursed garden. Like they say, misery loves company.*
>
> *But even though my brothers and I enjoyed seeing each other punished, we rarely ever ratted each other out. Honor among thieves, I*

suppose. It was all like a game to us, and tattling was grounds for disqualification. If you could drop Mom little hints along the way and manipulate her into discovering the wrongdoings of one of the others, then their punishment really became your victory. Which is why the time when Tommy busted the TV was so frustrating.

I knew he did it. Mom knew he did it. Heck, even the mailman knew he did it. But knowing and proving are two different things.

Billy was away at college, and I had accompanied Mom on one of her weekend trips to speak at various colleges throughout the country. We came back to a house that looked as if Eminem's newest music video had just been filmed in the family room. And the kitchen. AND the backyard. It was trashed.

Mom gave Tommy the talk that by then we all knew by heart, and he received his sentence within seconds of her walking through the door.

Thoroughly satisfied by the day's events, I decided to celebrate by kicking back and parking myself in front of my old friend, the television. I flipped it on from the comfort of the couch (whoever invented the remote control deserves his own national monument)—except it didn't flip on. I tried again: nothing. Dismayed and more than a little frustrated, I picked my way through the remains of Tommy's festivities to investigate, only to discover that someone had transported Lake Michigan to my den, with the TV at its dead center.

Except the TV wasn't just sitting in a pool of water; rather, it seemed to have gone for a bit of a swim. Indeed, there were traces of water from the top of it all the way down its back. This was no small matter, as this was a good-sized television set, back in the days when they built the glass screen out of the same stuff the local mob boss uses for his apartment windows.

When confronted about it, Tommy denied any involvement or knowledge (it always took us awhile to admit defeat). After Mom interrogated further (she was never one to give up), Tommy came up with a possible—if not plausible—theory: the dog peed on it. The dog in question was a miniature poodle who was barely even eye-level with one's knees, and the TV was a good five feet high.

The mental image was priceless. We all pictured Scamp, this little ball of fur, getting a running start and leaping into the air in slow motion, lifting his leg, and letting loose with his bladder at the perfect time as he arched over the top of the television, then smacking into the wall.

Whether she was too taken aback by the outrageous theory or too tired from her well-traveled weekend, Mom didn't bother pressing the matter. Tommy's punishment had already been decided, which is what was important. But not to me. My TV was broken, and the only explanation anyone had to offer was that the tiny dog peed on it. To this day I have no idea what happened to that TV, and I suspect it's one secret Tommy intends to take to the grave.

What, you may ask, possessed me to leave a sixteen-year-old home by himself on a Friday night? I rarely did it and should never have done it. It's the single mom's dilemma. After all, there was only one of me; it's only for one night; and he is sixteen years old for heaven sakes, old enough to be left alone for a single night. But I knew better. He wasn't—none of them were.

In hindsight I should have had a hard and fast rule that none of my boys could stay home alone for even one night. I should have had someone stay with them whenever this happened or had them stay the night at a friend's.

Even though he used to beg me to let him stay alone on occasion, today my son Stuart is absolute that no high school kid should ever be left alone at night. No good can come from it, he says. And he should know.

As one single parent to another, don't leave your kids alone at night or for long periods of time in the day, especially on a weekend. Find another solution and prevent the many problems that arise when kids are left to their own devices.

My Boys Brought Out the Best in Me

My youngest was a shy, quiet, hesitant child, unlike his brothers, and he stayed close by my side. But he was my Babe, so I thought nothing of it. What I didn't know was that he suffered from anxiety; I learned this when he was eleven.

I should have figured it out years earlier. To be precise, I should have realized it when he was in third grade. He had skipped second grade—a decision his first-grade teacher and I had made reluctantly. He was bored in school and tested ready for third, which was the starting grade at his brothers' all-boys school. I loved the idea of having all three of my boys at the same school and thought it would be especially good for Stuart. What I didn't know was just how tough life was about to get for my youngest.

When we arrived at school that first day, Stuart froze. He couldn't bring himself to go into the classroom. It took an enormous amount of coaxing to get him in the door. His teacher, Reed Armstrong, was a family friend, not to mention a world-renowned sculptor and the most remarkable educator I've ever met. We both agreed Stuart would be fine once he felt comfortable, and Reed worked hard to make that happen.

Stuart excelled as a student, loved Mr. Armstrong, and had lots of friends. But none of that seemed to matter. Every morning, as we drove to school, I would watch this seven-year-old become increasingly withdrawn and worried. The poor kid could hardly talk by the time we pulled up in front of the school, and no amount of assurance would help.

After weeks of struggling to get him to go into his classroom, Stuart and I came up with a system that worked. It still wasn't easy for him, but he could do it if we kept to the routine.

I would walk him down the hill to the log cabin that held the third and fourth grades. Stuart would reluctantly go into his classroom and sit at his desk, which was next to the window—a seat assignment I worked out with his teacher. I would stand outside the window where he could see me. Once seated, he'd hold up five fingers and I'd know he wanted me to wait five minutes before leaving. After a few minutes I would put up one finger. He would counter with two. This would go on until he signaled it was okay for me to leave—or until I nearly froze to death and begged him to release me.

I expected this arrangement to last a few weeks—just until he adjusted to his new environment. But I figured out that it had nothing to do with that; it was about me. He couldn't leave me. For the better part of two years I stood outside that child's classroom—in snow, rain, or shine—counting down fingers.

It was crazy, and before I had children, I would have dismissed any nutty mother who catered to her kids like that. But once I had my own, all that changed; I would do anything to make their path through life a little easier. They had to do the heavy lifting, but I would always be ready to help if they found the going too tough. I didn't care how I looked or what people thought. I was going to be there for my boys, doing what I could to help them through the hard times.

Stuart's condition—later diagnosed as separation anxiety—was something I couldn't understand. I had no experience with it or knowledge of it. I only knew that my son was struggling and that I had needed to help him get through it. I didn't know then—and I don't know today—if our solution was the best. I only knew it was *my* best—and that it worked.

Stuart went off to fifth and sixth grade without issue and was doing well in seventh when his father died. This tragedy triggered a severe reaction that left this shy eleven-year-old kid physically ill at the thought of separating from me. It took twelve tough months to find the expert who knew what the problem was, could explain it to us, and was able to put Stuart on a path to full recovery.

To watch a child struggle every day with the simplest of tasks, ones we take for granted, is gut wrenching. As a mom I worried constantly what would become of this boy. How would he cope with life's sharp turns? Then, when he was nineteen, Stuart had to make a decision that would take him away from family and friends for several years; he had to decide if he would go on a mission for his church. For months he was paralyzed with a wave of ever-increasing anxiety. Then one day he pulled himself together, took one look at his inner fears, and defied them. He wasn't going to let them stop him from moving forward with his life. He would go on his mission. I had never seen such courage nor ever been so moved. I knew then that Stuart could face anything life threw his way.

Life can be so tough on kids. And if there's only one parent in their home, it's all the tougher. Your children need you to be there, right by their side, using all the tools in your possession to help them find their way. As you do, they will change you. You will become stronger, bolder, more patient, and a great deal more humble. Your heart will become so full of love it will ache, and if you're anything like me, you'll be more grateful for the gift of children than for anything else in your life.

They Made Me Laugh So Hard

I have never laughed as often or as hard as I have being a mom. Kids are simply the funniest human beings alive—and they have no idea how entertaining they are. On one occasion Stuart had me bent over with laughter, so much so that I lost all authority as a parent.

I'll let him tell the story:

My brothers and I fought all the time. All three of us having loud, obnoxious, dominant personalities meant that we rarely saw eye to eye, and our attempts at persuasion typically resulted in a royal rumble. Unfortunately, because Tommy and Billy were three and five years older than me, respectively, my engagements rarely ended well for me. I usually put up as much of a fight as a punching bag would on a bad day. To be totally honest, in all the battles throughout all the years, I can only think of one real victory I ever won, but this victory, as my Mom still says, wiped the slate clean. In one moment, after fourteen years of losses, I succeeded in evening the score with my brother Billy.

Billy is the first to admit that as a teenager he was disagreeable at best, and at worst he was one of the Four Horsemen of the Apocalypse. Me, however—I was a perfect angel. I could do no wrong, and in every brotherly skirmish, I was the victim—at least, that's the way I spun it.

At eighteen Billy was always busy applying for colleges, which, as anyone who has done it knows, is not the most relaxing thing one can do. There was a fight. How it started is anyone's guess, but it ended just like all the rest: Billy palming my thirteen-year-old head and keeping it at arm's length while I swung and swung and swung—and missed and missed and missed. When he finally got bored of my increasingly sloppy and frustrated attacks, he threw me across the room and went about his business.

Some people don't know what it's like to have a temper. Those people have likely never bumped their shin on the edge of the coffee table or cheered for LeBron James in the NBA Finals. I was so mad that I felt like I was going to explode. It was so frustrating to never, ever win a fight against my older brothers, and I yearned for revenge.

Billy left me on the floor to lick my wounds and regroup. After he'd left I too went about my business, whatever business a thirteen-year-old might have—play video games, run around with the dogs out back, check to see what friends were online. While doing the latter my moment of triumph began to take shape.

I sat down at the computer, spun the chair around a few times as imbeciles are apt to do, and faced the screen. What I saw was the most beautiful sight my eyes had yet to behold: Billy had left one of his college applications up. The grin on my face would have done even the Joker proud.

Faced with the question that all applications have, "What sets you apart from other applicants?" Billy understandably left the computer to gather his thoughts. Still grinning, I peered over my shoulder and listened carefully to make sure nobody was going to walk in on me in my moment of triumph. Confident that I was going to be left alone for ample time, I returned to the task at hand: explaining in great detail exactly what sets Billy apart from their other applicants.

In order to appreciate my efforts, you must first understand that my brother Billy was the most conservative teenager you would ever meet. Yes, more often than not his attitude was diabolical, but I can't remember ever hearing him even utter a curse word, much less engage in any of the following actions.

In five hundred words or less I recounted Billy's wild and crazy adventures as a male pimp. I described his drug habits and how he went from using to dealing. I explained that it was a gradual decline, a slippery slope that led him to his current lifestyle. Though starting with some self-deprecation, I quickly delved into the realm of self-loathing, and I—he—told the university, "Please do not accept me, I am not worth it." If revenge were a form of art, this was the Sistine Chapel. After refining and revising my draft, I stared at my masterpiece and hovered the cursor over the "Submit Application" button. I thought to myself, What am I doing? If I do this, there is no going back. He'll kill me. He'll actually kill me. My palms were sweating, my hand was shaking, but I was grinning like a madman. CLICK. "Thank you for showing interest in our university." No, thank YOU.

Time passed, and I was still alive. Nobody even mentioned it. It was almost insulting—to have crafted such a masterpiece and get no recognition for it. But hey, at least I was alive, so I let it go. I moved on. I almost even forgot about it. Almost.

Months passed. Then one day after school I was sitting in the den reading a magazine, minding my own business, when I heard Billy talking to Mom in the kitchen. "Remember that university I applied to? I still haven't heard back from them," he told her. She told him to give them a call and that she was sure there was just a *misunderstanding. I could feel the corners of my mouth turn up in-voluntarily as I heard him go upstairs to make the call. I finished the page I was on and flipped to the next one, reveling in what I knew was about to happen.*

The sound of him stomping down the stairs at full speed was music to my ears. He related his conversation with the admissions office to Mom. He had asked about his application, and they had re-sponded, "You're that male pimp guy, right?" Billy was not happy. He was shouting out accusations, insisting it was one of Tommy's friends who did it, to which Mom simply said that was ridiculous— Tommy's friends couldn't pull off a stunt like that. I rose from my seat and calmly walked into the room, almost on cue, as Billy said, "Then who?"

Absorbed in the dilemma at hand, neither of them noticed me until I chimed in. "I did it."

"What did you do, Stuart?" my mom asked. "What exactly did you do?" I gave her the details, even though I knew it meant a swift retribution that would not end well for me. But as I expected death, I was instead met with a shocked brother and a hysterical mother. I don't think I have seen my mom laugh so hard. Billy, eyes wide, mouth wider, demanded she punish me. In the few breaths she man-aged to take between fits of laughter, she tried her best to sound seri-ous and to scold me. She failed—miserably.

In the end, not only did I commit the single greatest act of revenge ever committed by a thirteen-year-old, but I also did so (mostly) with-out repercussion. Billy didn't kill me and Mom didn't punish me— —or I already had so many overlapping groundings that it didn't matter. As a matter of fact, Billy never laid a hand on me again after that. In one fell swoop I tied the score after thirteen years of beatings, and let me tell you, it felt good.

What Stuart did was nothing short of outrageous. I knew that. And he needed to be held responsible. But I couldn't stop laughing. Never in all my days did I think Stuart had it in him to write such a thing and then send it to a school—a church-affiliated one, no less! It was too much for me. I laughed so hard and for so long that I lost all authority. There was nothing I could do to the kid after all that laughing.

But I could help Billy. The next day I called the school and told them that although the unseemly application came from his e-mail account, Billy had nothing to do with it. It was a prank, I said. (I didn't tell them it was another son who had pulled this little stunt off—it would have reflected badly on the family.) The problem was resolved, and a few weeks later Billy was attending the school.

And Now They Make Me Look So Good

My boys, now in their twenties, call me several times a week. We talk politics, religion, and, of course, movies. And we still love to share a good story. We keep up on one another's lives, vacation together in the summer, and try to spend some of the holidays together. We ask one another for advice, talk through professional decisions, and support each other in good and bad times. In short, we are still a family.

At the time of this writing, Billy is in his final year at Stanford Law School. He is married to Morgan, and they have two children, Eva and Will. Tommy is working as an analyst for an investment firm in Milwaukee. He is married to Kira, and they have one and a half children, Isaiah and who knows what (maybe Bay—it can be a boy's name too, you know). Stuart is finishing up college in Provo, Utah.

My sons chose great wives. Morgan and Kira are not only wonderful partners for my sons, but they are also spectacular moms. I love them like daughters, and because they are the mothers of my grandchildren, I treat them like queens. As for the grandbabies—there aren't words enough to describe the joy those little ones bring into my life.

I watch Billy and Tommy with their children, being the fathers that they never had, and my heart bursts with happiness. Stuart looks forward to his opportunity to be a husband and father, and I am certain he will be equally committed.

In spite of living in three different states, the boys are constantly in touch with one another. They are best friends. Tommy even talks about living close to his brothers one day. I don't know if that will ever work out, but I do know they'll always be there for one another.

My boys have become the men they were meant to be—I am certain of this. Each one is impressive in his own right. I know all too well the challenges they faced and the difficulties they overcame, and it makes me all the more amazed. I couldn't be more proud of these boys of mine, and am honored to call them my sons. Quite frankly, they make me look good.

The Bottom Line

Stuart recently told me that our family is different from others. He explained how he came to this conclusion. For years now he has been telling his friends stories about us, and invariably they are astounded. Maybe Stuart's right, we are different, I don't know. But what I do know is that although life in our home was definitely wild and crazy at times, it was always full of family and packed with fun.

Stuart loves his family, as do his brothers, and he talks about his childhood with the same sense of excitement and pleasure with which I speak of mine. And every time he does, it warms my heart. I did my best all those years, and it was enough. I gave my boys a childhood as good as the one I had. I put them first in my life and I kept them there—just as my dad and mom did for me.

I loved my kids and I loved my life with them. I was a single mom, solely responsible for my three boys. It wasn't what I signed up for, it wasn't what I wanted, but it's what life handed me. The responsibility was huge, the challenge overwhelming, but being a single mom was the greatest role I ever had or ever will have.

It's a twenty-four-hour-a-day job with no overtime. So where's the joy, you might ask? It is all around you. Just look for it and never let a day pass without feeling it. You'll find it in their smiles and in the tears you wipe away, in their funny expressions and in their hugs and kisses, in their favorite things and in the depth of their love for you. You'll feel the joy when they wake and when they sleep, when they struggle and when they succeed. And it will flood your home when you spend time with them—and your heart when you recall the memories. It's Rule #8: "Love being your kids' mom." Because it's the best job you'll ever have—and the most important.

Chapter Nine

My Eight Rules for Single Parenting

There is so much written and spoken that suggests single parents can't succeed. Our children, they tell us, are more likely to be low achievers, suffer depression, abuse drugs and alcohol, be sexually promiscuous, and drop out of school. There is more, but you get the point. There is no question—the statistics are disturbing.

But numbers don't tell our story. We do. We are moms. We make the difference for our kids—we give them what they need to defy these odds. We write the story of our families and we do it with our lives.

Single moms *can* succeed—and you must. We are talking about our children here! There is no other option. It's the most important job you'll ever do, so put your heart, mind, and soul into it and don't let anyone tell you that you can't do it. For the sake of your kids, reach deep inside yourself and find the strength, courage, and tenacity to be the mom they need.

The first step is to accept all the responsibility—and to hold yourself accountable to the task. Then give it everything you have. Change your life and make whatever sacrifices are needed to put your kids first in your life. It is tough going it alone, but you are a mom fighting for her children—and there's no one tougher than that.

I have eight rules for single moms. They work for all parents, but when you're raising kids on your own, there's no getting around any one of them. Every rule is essential if your goal is to succeed. So commit yourself to the course, the whole course, and put your kids on the path to becoming the men and women they were meant to be.

RULE #1:
YOU'RE A SINGLE MOM—TAKE CHARGE

It doesn't matter how you got here, how traumatic the trip has been, or how discouraged you are. What matters is that you are *now* a single mom. In this role you must succeed. Your kids are depending on it. So don't waste time. Walk away from that other life and leave the baggage behind. Throw yourself into the world of single parenting. It's going to take every bit of your strength, your energy, and your time to be the parent your kids need. So don't hold back. Give them your all.

It's time to stop thinking about the past and to start thinking about your kids. Take charge of your life, so you can take charge of theirs. There is no one your kids need more than you. Their lives hinge on you getting it together. They need to know you will figure it all out, make it work, and always be there for them.

You're the head of your family. Yes, the responsibility is enormous, as is the challenge. But you can do it; never think otherwise. Believe in yourself. Be strong. Be proud. You're a single mom. Take charge and never let anyone or anything come between you and your kids.

RULE #2:
LET THEIR DAD BE THEIR DAD

Give your kids every opportunity to have a close and healthy relationship with their father. It is unequivocally one of the most important things you can do for them. Kids know instinctively that their dad belongs in their life, and they desperately want him there. What's more—they need him there.

The evidence is overwhelming and indisputable. Children who live with both parents are far more likely to thrive than those who don't. So if your kids, for whatever reason, have no dad in their home, do everything you can to give them the next best thing—their dad in their lives.

No matter what you think of him, do what is right for your kids. Never bad-mouth their dad. Don't tell them anything that would make them think less of him or feel bad about him. But do tell them good things about him so they are comfortable openly loving him in their own home. Then do all in your power to see that they spend time with him. Right behind time with you, it's the greatest gift you can give them.

Ancillary to Rule #2:
Compensate for the Lack of a Dad in the Home
Kids learn so much and develop so well when they are raised in a loving two-parent family. You can't give your children that—not now—but you can and must compensate for the lack of a dad in their home. Find good two-parent families and strong male role models, and make them part of your kid's world. Through their example these friends can give your children an understanding and appreciation of the indispensable role of husband and father—and teach them priceless lessons that come with this knowledge.

RULE #3:
PUT YOUR KIDS FIRST

Here's the bottom line to raising kids as a single mom: the kids need you—your time, your energy, your heart, your guidance, your understanding, your discipline—they need all of you. Just being nearby doesn't cut it. They have to know they belong to you, that they are the center of your world. They need to be able to lean on you for strength, to feel secure and unafraid because you're their mom and will never let them down. That kind of trust doesn't come easily; it requires constant sacrifice. There is no other way. If you are committed to doing everything for your kids—if you are determined to give them a chance to beat the odds—then you have to put your kids first in your life. And not just sometimes—always.

Forget about blocks of time for yourself and high-powered jobs; forget about dating and romantic getaways. Spend your evenings and weekends with your kids. Give them a deep sense of belonging that comes with being part of a strong family. This doesn't just happen; it takes living life together as a family—and only you can do that for your kids.

Do whatever it takes to put your kids first in your life. Then keep them there. Don't hesitate and don't hold back—give yourself to them. Your kids can make it; they can thrive—but not without you—all of you.

RULE #4:
STRIP PARENTING DOWN TO THE BASICS

Single moms need to forget all thoughts of perfection, and toss out "nearly perfect" while you're at it. It doesn't exist in our world. You need a new game plan, an updated, streamlined version, one that works for you and your kids.

You're one person with the job of two. It's not easy, but you can do it if you give yourself a chance. Strip parenting down to the basics. It's the only way to know for certain that you're focusing your time and energy on the important stuff—and that's what being a single mom is all about.

Cut expectations down to size. Throw overboard the high, unrealistic ideals of the past. Keep only what matters and get rid of the rest. Simplify, prioritize, and chop until you find the right balance for your family. Scrap the nonessentials and give your kids what they need the most—time with you.

RULE #5:
GIVE YOUR KIDS A HOME TO LOVE

The home you give your kids is as important to them as the air they breathe and the food they eat. It needs be like a giant security blanket wrapped tightly around them, providing them at every stage of development with a powerful sense of belonging and a guaranteed refuge from the outside world.

For kids to thrive, their home has to be a place where they feel the comfort and confidence that comes with being part of something bigger than themselves. Surrounded by loved ones they learn they're not alone in this world, that there'll always be someone close by to teach them what they need to know, to help them through the tough days and to pick them up when they fall down. They learn their home isn't just where they live—it's where they belong because it's where their family lives.

Give your kids a home to love—a family-centered, magical place where they live together with you, talking and laughing, playing and sharing, loving and caring. Put televisions, computers, and game systems in a family room. Drive your kids out of their bedrooms and into family space. Time together is what makes families, and this happens in the home. It's your job to see it happens in yours.

RULE #6:
BE THEIR PARENT, NOT THEIR FRIEND—
SET RULES AND ENFORCE THEM

Single moms have to establish—and enforce—rules. You can't avoid either step. One doesn't work without the other. There's no escaping it. Your kids will have plenty of friends in their lifetime, but only one mom. You need to be their parent—friend doesn't cut it.

Expectations and limits—and enforcement—are vital to your kids. Simply talking to them is totally and completely inadequate. In fact, it's nothing but a cop-out. Your kids need absolutes from you, not chit-chat. Give them clearly defined rules, explain the driving principles behind them, and tell them that as a member of your family they're expected to live by those rules. Then enforce them and never stop.

Good parenting requires consistent and fair enforcement of established rules; single parenting demands it. If you want your kids to succeed, you have to be relentless when it comes to keeping them in line. With rules, kids thrive; without them they get lost. Do what is best for your kids. Be their parent, not their friend—set rules and enforce them. It's what your kids need, and no matter how tough it is, it's what you'll do if they are first in your life.

RULE #7:
ESTABLISH FAMILY TRADITIONS—
MAKE TIME WITH YOUR KIDS' ROUTINE IN YOUR HOME

Family traditions are a single parent's best friend. They are the most powerful tools in your possession. There is nothing that works as well to guide and direct your family. They ground your kids and give their lives structure. Your children see and feel a strong, undeniable attachment to their family, which creates within them an invaluable sense of belonging.

Traditions establish a familiar and special world for your kids. This is their life—it's what they do and who they are. They grow comfortable with the routine and secure in their roles. The traditions you choose for your family will define the culture in which your kids are raised, give direction to their lives, and leave them with precious memories that will last a lifetime.

The traditions of family dinner and church attendance are two of the most effective parenting tools available. Numerous studies have found that they both have immeasurable benefits for your kids. As one single mom to another: do right by your kids—eat with them, go to church with them, and establish other family traditions that put you together with your kids for quality time every single day. Establish family traditions—make time with your kids' routine in your home. Then watch the magic flow.

RULE #8:
LOVE BEING YOUR KIDS' MOM

As a single mom, appreciate what you have—kids who love you, a home full of family, years packed with great memories. It's a good life, so live it right and enjoy it to its fullest. Let your kids see how much you love your life with them. Let them know how grateful you are to be their mom, how proud you are to call them your own.

Every day look for the joy of being their mom. You'll find it in their smiles and in the tears you wipe away, in their funny expressions and in their hugs and kisses. You'll feel the joy when they wake and when they sleep, when they struggle and when they succeed. And it will overwhelm you when they turn and say "I love you."

Raising kids alone is enormously challenging—and at times brutally difficult. But it's the most amazing job you'll ever have—and the most crucial. Don't let it slip by without feeling the overwhelming joy that is yours if you do it right. There is no greater accomplishment in life than being a good parent. So be the mom your kids need.

Nothing will fill your heart, your home, or your life with more joy.

Epilogue

Stuart Buchanan Jackson

When Mom first started writing this book, she often wondered how well it would do once it was published. What I told her surprised even myself: "If it only sells one copy, if that copy gives that single parent the hope and strength not to give up, then it was all worth it." I hadn't realized until then how deeply I felt about the matter. It all hit me in that one brief exchange: where would I be if Mom had given up?

Where would I be if she hadn't been able to wipe the tears from her eyes during those early years after Dad left? Who would I be if she had decided that it was too much work to raise me and my brothers alone? What kind of life would I have lived?

Those questions terrify me. But the thing is that I don't have to wonder because she *didn't* give up on us; she *didn't* give in to despair. She took life one day at a time, learning the lessons day by day that she has now shared with you here. My brothers and I knew that she was doing her best, and that knowledge made all the difference.

I can't tell you how to raise your kids. But what I can tell you is that *you will* make an impact on their lives that will never end. Good parenting isn't easy (I know because I was the one making it not easy for my mom), but it is worth it. You may not see it at first, but all that love and hard work will take root within the hearts of your children, and it will grow until it becomes the foundation for the rest of their lives. I can tell you that because of who I am today, in contrast to who I was as a kid.

My dad was a stranger to me for the better part of my life. On visits he often preferred to take out only my two older brothers, which is understandable, as it would be difficult to spend quality time with two young children while also looking after an infant.

Though Dad would come visit us a couple times a year in Virginia, Mom also let my older brothers fly out to California for a week every summer by themselves, one at a time, for some quality time with Dad. I remember watching them come back from those trips; I had never seen my brothers as happy as they were when they'd just spent a week with him. I would look at them and wonder what it was about this man that changed them, really changed them from who they were almost into who they were supposed to be. I would wonder what it would be like if I could spend a week with my dad.

Finally, when I was around nine years old, Mom decided that I was old enough to fly out to California alone. I was both thrilled and mortified. I had spent weekends at friends' houses—but a whole week with a man I barely knew?

Saying goodbye to Mom at the airport was painful, but once I was on the plane it was like an adventure. Flight attendants doted on me, new and interesting people shared even more interesting stories with me, and I got to play my Gameboy to my heart's content. (I wasn't complaining.)

I remember that first time that I disembarked from the plane—seeing my dad there and the look on his face. That was the first time I ever knew that he loved me. He threw his arms around me so tight that I could barely breathe, and what little breath I found was full of Old Spice aftershave (the man had to shave constantly; his five o'clock shadow put Moses to shame).

That week he took me to Disneyland, Universal Studios, Sea World. It was incredible. But not because of what we saw or the things we did—it was incredible because I was with my dad.

But that week ended. During the drive to the airport I couldn't talk, couldn't swallow. I would glance over at him from the front seat, trying to take a picture of his face with my mind, trying to immortalize him in my memory. When he would look over at me, I would glance away, embarrassed and afraid that he would notice my apprehension. I wanted to be big and strong for him rather than some whimpering baby. But I was neither big nor strong; I was nine and terrified—terrified that when I left, I wouldn't remember his face or, worse, that he wouldn't remember me.

When we got to the gate, I looked at the door to the plane as if it were the gates of hell. I turned and threw my arms around his neck and cried and cried and cried, and I begged him to let me stay for just another day or two. I did this because I didn't want to leave and I'd miss him *so* much. I needed to tell him those things, but more than that, I needed to hear him say them back. But he didn't.

"I love you. I love you so much. Please don't make me go," I told him over and over again. But he didn't listen. He made me go. And for five hours flight attendants tried to dote on me, interesting strangers tried to tell me even more interesting stories, and I tried to play my Gameboy to my heart's content. But all I could do was try not to forget his face.

This story repeated itself for a couple years, with every summer visit to California being the same: Disneyland, Universal Studios, Sea World, Legoland, Dad. They all started with big hugs and Old Spice, and they all ended with me needing to hear him say that he loved me and that he'd miss me. It never happened.

But when I was eleven, as he drove me back to the airport where my heart would break like it always did, he told me that he wanted me to fly out and visit him at Christmastime. That was the closest he ever came to telling me what I needed to hear him say. That was in August.

Fast forward to October of that year. My cousin-turned-best-friend Anton and his family were visiting us. You know those kids who seem to understand each other so well that they can communicate without speaking? We were those kids. I remember every single detail of that night. Anton and I grabbed our dinner and sat down in the den to watch some TV. The phone rang. Sometimes I think that I felt the weight of that ring as I sat there making a mashed potato volcano.

My Uncle Buck came into the den and told me that my mom wanted to see me upstairs. Being in no hurry to face the punishment for some as-yet-undiscovered crime, I slowly finished my dinner. Before I could take two bites Uncle Buck came back in, and in a stern but oddly caring voice said "Now." I put down my plate and went up the stairs.

Mom was sitting on the bed with Billy on one side of her and motioned for me to sit on the other side. Tommy was in the chair at the computer facing us.

Sometimes I think we all knew—Billy, Tommy, and me. For one thing, it was completely quiet, which for us required nothing short of divine intervention.

Mom started to cry and then stated simply, "Your father passed away. I'm so sorry."

Everything that followed is a blur. All I remember is feeling my heart break and saying, "So I'm not going to get to see him at Christmas, am I?"

My world shattered that night—as did those of my brothers—and we each spent the next few years picking up the pieces in our own way.

The hardest part for me was understanding and accepting that I would never hear those words from Dad. All my fears had come true: I would never see his face again, and I would surely forget it. I wouldn't ride on his shoulders at Disneyland when my feet got tired, staring at the bald spot on top of his head. I wouldn't feel the air escape my lungs when he hugged me too tight, getting a whiff of Old Spice when I would finally catch my breath.

He let me down, and now he had no chance of making it up to me. I was a broken-hearted eleven-year-old.

Mom didn't understand fully then how we each felt. I never told her that before I was even a teenager all my greatest fears had come true. But she continued to do her best. In the end her love and diligence and sacrifice filled the gap my father left. She never stopped showing us how much she loved us, never stopped smacking us upside the head, and never stopped *believing* in us.

Now I'm twenty-three. I could tell you about the things I've accomplished or the lives that Billy and Tommy have made for themselves, but what matters most is who we are, and we are our mother's children. Her efforts shaped our lives, just as your efforts will shape the lives of your children. But if Mom ever taught me anything, it's to enjoy the journey: learn, laugh, love—and all that jazz.

Thanks, Mom. For everything.

Acknowledgments

There are friends, and then there are those special people who become part of your extended family. Ed Markovich is one of the latter. I have known him most of my life, and my boys have known him all of theirs. Whether it was holidays, special family events, or just a day at MGM Studios, Ed was there for my kids—a true uncle to them. When we spoke by phone to get caught up, he always asked about the kids and would invariably end these calls with the words, "Bay, you have to write a book!" Ed never let the idea travel far from my mind, and thanks to his years of encouragement, this book was written.

Then there is my agent, Alice Martell, who has been a believer in me and in this project from the get-go, and she made it all happen. Her immensely constructive criticism and powerful encouragement were invaluable every step of the way, and I am deeply grateful for both. No writer could ever ask for more—nor could a friend.

I also want to thank my good friend Sharon Korchnak, who was never more than a phone call away. She was always ready to help with research and formatting—and never failed to pass along loads of much-needed encouragement.

I am indebted to Kristin Larsen, my executive assistant, who ran my office while I was off writing. I simply could not have finished this book without her and am incredibly thankful for her steady hand at the wheel this past year.

I must also thank my boys Billy and Tommy for the words they wrote that added enormously to this book. And I am especially grateful to my son Stuart for the stories he contributed, the editing he did, and his wonderful epilogue. And I thank all three of them for giving me a life to remember and plenty of material about which to write.

All good books must pass through the hands of a good editor, and I was extremely fortunate to have Katie McHugh as mine. The experience was something close to shock treatment, but Katie forced me through the editing process, and the result was a greatly improved book. I must also thank Christine Marra, my project manager, for the friendly but efficient manner in which she guided me through the final stages of production.

I usually wrote at home, but my son and his family moved in with us in June and stayed until mid-September. With two grandbabies in the next room, concentrating on work was impossible. So I became a squatter at the local Starbucks, Panera's, California Tortilla, and Foster's Grill. I would sit and type for four to five hours at a time and then move to the next establishment, where I would work for several more hours. One night the manager of the California Tortilla asked me if the music was too loud. "I don't want anything to disturb our in-house author," he told me. I will always remember the kindness of these employees; they always made me feel welcomed as I worked next to them day after day.

Lastly I want to thank my husband, Walt. We were married only ten months when I began this project. Although the book consumed much of my time and energy for nearly a year, his patience and support never wavered. Words can't express my appreciation.

Index

About the Author

Bay Buchanan is a political strategist, pundit, and mother. She served as United States Treasurer in the Reagan administration and has been a senior adviser to Pat Buchanan, Tom Tancredo, and Mitt Romney. Named one of the top ten most influential conservative women by the Clare Boothe Luce Policy Institute, she is currently president of The American Cause as well as a political analyst frequently seen on CBS, CNN, MSNBC, and Fox News. A native of Washington, DC, Buchanan lives in Oakton, VA. You can contact her at BayandHerBoys @gmail.com.